Jazz Generations

To my family
for being an inspiration throughout my musical life

son Zan and daughters Cheryl, Veda, and Crystal
grandchildren Shatara, Roshanda, Frederic, William, Aundrey,
Brandon, Andrew, Christopher
great-grandchildren Dominick, Raven, and Dante
sister Doris
and
niece Barbara Ann

Jazz Generations

A life in American music and society

Buddy Collette
with
Steven Isoardi

Continuum
London and New York

Continuum
Wellington House, 125 Strand, London WC2R 0BB
370 Lexington Avenue, New York, NY 10017–6503

First published in Great Britain in 2000 by Continuum by arrangement with Bayou Press Ltd

British Library Cataloguing-in-Publication Data

A catalogue record for this book is available from the British Library.

ISBN 0-8624-4720-1 (hardback)
ISBN 0-8624-4721-X (paperback)

Library of Congress Cataloging-in-Publication Data

Collette, Buddy, 1921–
  Jazz generations : a life in American music and society / by Buddy Collette with Steven Isoardi.
    p. cm.
  Includes bibliographical references and index.
  ISBN 0-8624-4720-1—ISBN 0-8624-4721-X (pb)
    1. Collette, Buddy. 2. Jazz musicians—United States—Biography. I. Isoardi, Steven. II. Title.

ML419.C635 A3 2000
788.7′165′092—dc21
[B]

99-089418

Typeset by Paston PrePress Ltd, Beccles, Suffolk
Printed and bound in Great Britain by Biddles Limited, Guildford and Kings Lynn

Contents

Preface

Steven Isoardi

Before I had the opportunity to meet Buddy Collette, I'd known of him through his numerous recordings, especially the early Chico Hamilton Quintet albums, local appearances, and Charles Mingus' semi-autobiography, semi-fantasy *Beneath the Underdog*.[1] When I began studying saxophone with Bill Green in 1987, I learned more of the man and artist from his colleague and close friend of forty years. Even so, I was not prepared for the range of his contributions and involvements, musical and otherwise, that I was subsequently to learn of during the course of a collaboration that now spans more than a decade.

This autobiography grew from an extensive oral history interview I did with Buddy for the UCLA Oral History Program's Central Avenue Sounds project. When Dale Treleven, the director of the UCLA Program, and I started organizing the project and prioritizing our list of potential interviewees, it became evident that Buddy should be our first contributor. Talking to a variety of people, we learned that his authority as a musician, history of progressive political involvement, and his qualities of character gave him such a standing within the musical – not just jazz – and African American, Latino and Anglo communities that his support and participation would stamp an immediate and definitive validation on the project. Such was the case. A typical response from prospective interviewees was, "Buddy's involved? Oh, okay." Or when discussing the legal agreement used by the Oral History Program, it was not unusual to hear, "Buddy signed it? Yeah, give me the pen."

---

[1] [Charles] Mingus. *Beneath the Underdog*. Edited by Nel King. New York: Alfred A. Knopf, Inc., 1971.

Buddy agreed to be my first interviewee and we started taping in July 1989. He proved to be a true raconteur. After I pressed the RECORD button and asked the lead question, he took over and the stories came pouring out, session after session, over five months and through sixteen cassettes. Buddy is a wonderful story-teller and he relishes unfolding a tale. But he is much more: an African American griot whose stories always infuse history with insights, lessons, and morals about people and events. In every experience there is some-thing of value to learn – something to pass on to a larger and future audience, that shapes his perceptions and recollections.

As I worked with Buddy on this book from the end of 1996 and into 1998, I was also continuing with other Central Avenue Sounds interviews for the UCLA project. Invariably, each new interviewee would add more stories of Buddy, ranging from various union activities to combating Latino-black violence and promoting music education in the schools. There seemed to be no end to his involve-ments and contributions. I soon realized that it would be a Sisyphian task to document all of them, and reset the more modest goal of covering those defining moments essential to his story and to an understanding of the magnitude of his achievements.

Buddy's authority rests on many varied musical and social life-long involvements and accomplishments. He is one of the few musicians to achieve an international reputation – as a multi-instrumentalist and as a composer – while remaining in Los Angeles and not seeking the richer jazz pastures of New York. His command of the saxophone, clarinet and flute instrument families is author-itative, and his compositions and improvisations always have been fresh, richly melodic, and never repetitious. As a mentor, confidant, friend and/or teacher, Buddy has positively impacted the lives of generations of musicians including Sonny Criss, Eric Dolphy, Charles Lloyd, Big Jay McNeely, Charles Mingus, Frank Morgan, and James Newton.

He has also combined his life as a musician with a deep involvement in the social struggles of his time. Buddy is a member of that generation who grew up in a segregated United States and was politically transformed by the experience of the Second World

War and its immediate aftermath. By the late 1940s Buddy had initiated the fight to end segregation in the American Federation of Musicians. That struggle began a battle against social injustice that Buddy has continued up to the present within his union and the Hollywood studios, as well as within the African American and other communities of Los Angeles.

The life histories of artists such as Buddy Collette are important not only as a record of their personal journeys, but also as windows into the communal roots and development of black culture. The most cursory glance through a listing of black artists' biographies reveals the contributions of many black communities throughout the country and the co-existence of many musical styles and influences. New York has been a destination for many musicians, and certainly a media center, but most arrive shaped by their various communities and having left behind many talented and artistically productive musicians who chose to remain there.

A few, such as Buddy, have managed to do both, providing an invaluable connection to both the musicians in their local communities, especially the younger ones emerging, and to those artists in the major centers who rely on a regular infusion of new talent and variety of musical experience from the source. Consequently, Buddy's story offers insights both into the world of black music from a national and international perspective, as well as from the fertile soil of local community experience. His committed and principled involvement in our society at so many levels – international, national, local, musical, and social – gives his life a meaning and significance beyond that of his chosen artistic field.

Acknowledgments

We started working on this autobiography by creating a rough draft based on the lengthy transcript of the Buddy Collette Interview in the UCLA Oral History Program's Central Avenue Sounds project. Consequently, we are indebted to the Program's director, Dale Treleven; to its organizer Alva Moore Stevenson; and to editors Alex Cline, Teresa Barnett, David Gist, and Vimala Jayanti, all of whom contributed to the creation of a superb interview transcript. The interview was made possible in part by the generous support of Lucille Ostrow.

An early inspiration was Viki King, who persistently urged that memories be put on tape. During the mid-1980s Elaine Cohen began preliminary work on the autobiography, which was instrumental in pushing in the direction of what has now become a full life-story.

A few dedicated, knowledgeable readers generously contributed their expertise, reading various drafts of this book. Many thanks to Richard Birkemeier, Dr. Art Davis, Viki King, Mimi Melnick, Lyle "Spud" Murphy, Phil Pastras, and Pat Willard for their professional skills and generous spirits.

Additional taping sessions required a substantial amount of transcribing. That arduous task was undertaken by Carole Moran and Suzanne Abril. We thank them for contributing their considerable talents.

Mimi Melnick contributed the invaluable index with her usual intelligence, diligence, accuracy, and graciousness. She continues to be an invaluable part of our jazz community.

Finally, our warmest thanks to Alyn Shipton of the Bayou Press for being so staunchly supportive, indeed, enthusiastic about this book, and to his colleagues at Continuum – a gracious and sympathetic staff whose professional talents have made this such a pleasurable experience.

Introductions

Buddy Collette is a musician *extraordinaire*, citizen of the world, humanitarian, musical philanthropist, and fearless fighter for the rights of musicians and all humans. His compassion for his fellow man is exceeded only by his love of music, especially Jazz, which is his natural heritage.

I first met Buddy fifty-eight years ago in 1942, while working in the Les Hite Orchestra. In the 1950s we shared an apartment on St. Andrews Place in Los Angeles. Throughout the years, we have worked together in various bands, including my orchestra and Buddy's own successful band. His long career has brought him many challenges and has rewarded him with countless successes, making him an international favorite.

There is no need for me to elaborate on the detailed contents of this autobiography. In reading *Jazz Generations*, you, the reader, will discover this remarkable man of our times. His 1956 album, *Man of Many Parts*, truly summarizes the essence of Buddy Collette. I am grateful to be a part of his life because not only is he an honored colleague, he is also my dear friend.

Gerald Wilson

Knowing each other, all of our musical lives,
And believing that – music is one of God's wills
            and God's will, will be done.
Buddy, that you have done.
      You've been blessed.
      Love you "B."

Chico Hamilton

1
Los Angeles beginnings

Family

I was born in Los Angeles, California in 1921, in Los Angeles General Hospital, and lived near Compton Avenue and Thirty-third Street. My parents weren't from Los Angeles, but they met here. Goldie Marie Dorris Collette, my mother, was from Kansas City, Kansas. When she was around thirteen, she lost her mother and with her sister, Opal, was put into a boarding school. They were raised by their father, Arthur Dorris, part of the time. To find better work opportunities, he moved the family to California around 1918, 1919.

My dad, Willie Collette, was from Knoxville, Tennessee, and was born in 1900. He might have been fifteen, sixteen or seventeen, when they came to California. In my dad's case, my grandmother, Matilda Collette, and grandfather, William Collette, again, decided it was just a better life-style in California; better in terms of the racial situation, jobs, and even the weather. So they moved to Los Angeles.

Mom and dad met when my mother and her family rented a house that was owned by my dad's parents, right behind their house. Dad's line was that he knew she was going to be his woman. He saw her walking and the light turned on: "Ah, that lady I'm going to get." That was his terminology. He saw this beautiful women, who was maybe three years older than him, and he knew exactly what he wanted. With my dad there was no in-between. He *knew* that this woman had gotten to him. So he sat at the piano and put all his energy into the few tunes he knew. Mom was curious and stood there listening to this piano player. She did like music and was a great singer, not a schooled one, but she sang in church and had a voice like a bird, very pretty.

1

We weren't rich, but we weren't that poor. Dad drove a garbage truck for the city, which was a great job at that time. He was a black man, the driver, and was very proud of that, and stayed neat in spite of that truck. People were throwing the trash and garbage in it, but he was king of the road. I was very proud of him, because he was sharp. He stayed clean, always came in and showered, put on the clothes. He wore the stickpins, the hat, a great suit, and always had a brand new car, like an Auburn Cord, the flashy low-cut cars with the convertible tops. There was a husband-and-wife dance team, Bloomfield and Greeley, that had a Cord with a nickel-plated hood that would just about blind us. That's where my dad was. He had the greatest personality and everybody loved him. In later years he would come to a party with me and charm the whole group. They'd forget about me and my musicians.

Mom and dad were both beautiful people, but they were like night and day. My mom had graduated from the Topeka Industrial and Educational Institute in May 1914, with a degree in cosmetology, which was unusual for a black woman at that time. Dad was more streetwise, probably had gone to school through the eighth or tenth grade, but never finished high school. He loved playing games. He and his buddies would add a thick wad of paper, cut to the size of bills, to twenty or thirty dollars, making it look like he might have had a few thousand. He was from a kind of street gang and he knew about gambling, probably pimping and the whole street scene, because of the people he hung around, one of whom was his brother, my Uncle Jimmy.

Uncle Jimmy owned a pool hall and Collette's Liquor Store, around Forty-second Street and Central Avenue, but he was mostly a gambler. At twenty years old he already had a heavy crowd around him, had new suits, a brand new Cadillac. When most people were making four or five dollars a day, he was pulling in a hundred. He was a player, one of those guys that had the knack, and awful sharp, always the classiest women around him. Every Christmas the family would meet for dinner at my grandmother's, and then we'd meet at my aunt's for New Year's Eve. Uncle Jimmy would always bring one

2

of the foxiest ladies you'd ever want to see. He must have been a hell of a gambler.

Dad and Jimmy grew up near Twenty-third and Central by the Newton Police Station. Two of their friends, the Goodlows, were nice guys and became police officers, while others, like the Bigelow boys, went a different direction. The Bigelows were wild, rough guys, stealing and selling tires, and into dope as well. One of them was killed by the police when they raided their house. The cops broke in as they were trying to flush the stuff down the toilet. One of them tried to swallow some pot and the officer choked him trying to get it. Many guys didn't want to work for a few dollars a day and were hustling through that period. Those were my dad's friends, but he was never that kind, never did much gambling. He had two sides: one was intrigued by all this action, and the other never did anything about it. He loved taking a cut of the action, but he couldn't go along with getting caught.

In the meantime, dad wanted us to be on our best behavior. When I was about five, one Sunday morning my mother and I went to Mr. Harrison's store, our neighborhood store just around the corner from where we lived. Walking around Mr. Harrison's, I noticed some apricots, ate one and put a few in my pocket. When we got home, mom told dad what I had done, but they didn't say anything to me. As we were having breakfast, there was a knock on the door. "We've come for Buddy Collette. We're the police and we're going to take him to jail." I'm listening to this and just dying. My dad goes to the door and says, "Please don't take him. He's a good boy and would never do that. I can't believe he stole the apricots." This went on for a little while, until dad closed the door and came back to breakfast. It wasn't the police, but a neighbor. My dad had set up the scene to teach me a lesson.

Dad was also very tight with money when it came to the rest of us. He'd leave a dollar for all of us for school lunch. Mom was always very quiet about it. She'd make rice, beans, potatoes, things that would stretch. When she said that we didn't have enough money to have milk, he'd say, "Well, I left you a dollar." He'd make you feel terrible asking for money. What he gave was never enough, but he always had plenty for himself. As a kid, I figured, "I'm going to learn to do something so I won't have to go to him." If you needed anything, he was the worst one to ask. Mom always tried to get him to take her out to breakfast once a week. He'd do it maybe once a month, and then he'd take her to the donut shop. She still wouldn't complain: "We went and had donuts and coffee this morning. At least he took me out." Then he'd go have lunch somewhere else with his friends. He wasn't starving and all the while cutting corners on her and on us.

Mom was so different from him, had so much heart, so much love and warmth for people, which was a great thing. She would always give you anything she had and would want to share all the time. When I'd bring my school friends home, whether they were white, Mexican, black, whatever, she'd say, "It's time for your food." I'd say goodbye to them and she'd interrupt, "No, you're not sending them home. You ask them to dinner." When I'd complain that we didn't have enough, she'd say, "You have to share what you have." If it was just a hamburger, that hamburger went down the middle for my little buddy.

In some ways my mom was much wiser than dad was, but he was sharp at fixing things and learning things, and he had almost total recall. He'd remember everything and was always criticizing and pointing things out to catch us. He could have been a fine lawyer, although he didn't have the educational qualifications. Mom was never critical, rather accepting, with life and nature. If somebody hit you over the head with a baseball bat and you came in crying, she'd just take care of you and then give you a big hug. You were back out to the game in no time. No panic. She had confidence.

Even though they weren't bickering all the time, I could see there was no warmth of communication and it does affect you. It hurts because you always want to have a close family. But they somehow got along and never complained. My mom shared a lot of her warmth with us, the kids. She was able to make us feel comfortable and never spoke out against him, ever. He would always stay out late, though never all night, coming in at four or five in the morning. Dad had his own rules: "I can do anything between nine and four in the

4

morning, but I will go home," and that's what he stood for, not staying away. It was not an unhappy childhood, but it wasn't a warm family. Most of the time it was just mom and us. When he'd come back, he could be critical. The kids didn't do this or that. You'd hear that from him, but he wouldn't participate much in family activities. Even to his last days, he never complimented me on my playing or career. Instead, he'd ask if I was making enough money, or if I needed some.

"Are you working? Are things working out for you? Need money or anything?"

He was that kind of dad and always more concerned with the practical aspects, how much money you were making. I would hear from other people: "He talks about you like you're the greatest in the world." But I'd never hear anything like that from him. Just before he died, he said, "I heard you play the flute. You sounded like a little bird." That was the biggest compliment I ever got from him. He knew when he liked it, but he could never share it. Charles Mingus, who always talked to my dad, would say, "Man, your dad is telling me all this stuff."

And I thought, "He never tells me anything."

But they trusted me and I wasn't any problem. Jackie Kelson, a dear friend of mine, was brought up in a setting with very strict parents. We both had a chance to work in Cee Pee Johnson's band, when we were about nineteen. Marshal Royal and Jack McVea had just left Cee Pee to go with Lionel Hampton's first band. It was a great job and paid about thirty-five dollars a week; my dad was making twenty-five dollars a week at the time. Jack's dad wouldn't let him take it. He wanted him to stay in school, go to college. My dad wasn't strict like that. He was too busy with his activities. He'd say, "Hey, I'm glad you got a job," not who's gonna be there and what are the girls like. They weren't putting any demands on me, and mom just said, "If you're my son, you're great enough for me. You don't have to prove anything." From early on that attitude helped me a lot. I did get the feeling, at ten, eleven, or twelve, that I wanted to be a musician and that it was only because I liked it. There was no pressure from them, that this is what I should be, or that this is what I should be constantly working toward. Mom would say, "Just keep playing those pretty sounds and you'll be fine."

I grew up with one brother, Pat, and one sister, Doris. Pat, who died in 1985, was two years younger than me and Doris is two years older. Doris was a beautician for a long time, until she gave it up and moved to California City. She was a piano player, but didn't do much with her music other than play for enjoyment. Pat became a disc jockey. When he was about thirty years old, he got a job at KNOB, which was mostly a jazz station. A good friend of mine, Amos Green, was there as well. Amos was always around jazz and even wore a saxophone strap sometimes just to pretend. Those guys weren't making a lot of money, but Pat loved it. He had a beautiful show called "Jazz Goes to Church," and he used "Come Sunday" by Duke Ellington and Mahalia Jackson as his theme song. My brother and my dad never got along too well, probably because they were quite a bit alike. But my dad liked me, because I was active and always doing things. My brother was a good talker, but most of the time he would do a little job here and there, and then take plenty of time off. My dad was like that, too, except when he had something going. When my dad took care of business, he took care of business.

My brother wanted to be like dad, out there in the street, and it worked against him. I didn't want that and never liked the street scene too much. I think my grandmother instilled that in me. She wanted you to be something. I only saw her once a week, when she paid for my piano lessons, but she definitely gave me the messages: "Watch out who you run with." "Don't do that." "Practice and you're going to go somewhere." I can still hear her voice saying those things. She had a recruitment poster for black soldiers from World War I hanging on a wall in her house that read: "A COLORED MAN IS NO SLACKER." My grandfather was strong too, a real quiet man, marvelous, but quiet. He was supposed to have had a bar when he was a younger man. He liked helping me and my sister by giving us work, so we could earn our own money.

I saw the wilder life through my dad and my uncle, and I wanted to be different than they were. Music was a challenge to me, to be able to say, "I know something. I can do something." I took after my

6

mother and grandmother's side of the family. My grandmother would say you have to go after it, and my mom always stood for truth and for people and good things. I felt that if I could just go by their teaching, then I'd come off very well.

For a long time after my mom died, dad worried about Pat, because my brother thought he was watching my dad, taking care of him, and my dad kept turning it around. "I don't know why he keeps hanging around me. I'd like him to go out and work." When my brother died first, that threw my dad, because you don't think that your kid's going to die before you. He was getting on in years and stayed confused after that. It was almost like: "What happened? I didn't get a chance to really talk to him." That rattled him, and he died a few months after my brother.

Growing up in Watts

We moved from Thirty-third Street and Compton Avenue in 1924 or 1925 to the Central Gardens area, which was Ninety-second Street south to about 100th Street, just above Watts. We lived at Parmelee Avenue and Ninety-sixth, and I went to the Ninety-sixth Street School, about four blocks away. There were other schools in that area, but they were for whites only, like South Gate Junior High and High Schools, which were on Firestone Boulevard near Alameda. There was a borderline there. You could walk past Alameda, but you'd feel like a stranger and you sure couldn't go to school over there. So I went to school in Watts.

The main street in Watts was 103rd Street. Most of the businesses were there and it had two theaters, the Linda and the Largo. The Linda Theatre, on 103rd near Compton Avenue, was not too well maintained, complete with holes in the walls and rats running through the place, and they showed cowboy films. The Largo was classy. It was near Wilmington and 103rd Street, could seat around three hundred people, and showed all the best films. They also had some live shows. For a few months my early band, that included Charles Mingus and Crosby Lewis, performed there during their

7

amateur nights. The place would be packed and we'd be out back in the alley at eight o'clock practicing for the nine o'clock amateur contest. It was great.

The area you grow up in is so important and this area had so much. We grew up in Watts, and there were all kinds of people there, all races: whites, blacks, Mexicans, Chinese, Japanese. Part of the reason was because it was a reasonble area, cheap, plenty of land. For maybe $1,000 or $2,000 you had a home. Houses were built mainly by the people who lived in them. My dad built our house and he did a good job. In the twenties Watts was developing as a little city and schools were being built. Nobody seemed to have a lot of money then, but we had food on the table.

The various ethnic groups didn't all live together. You might have whites on a few blocks here and then Japanese on a few blocks there, but the distances were so small and everybody was together in the schools. I remember in my graduation classes kids of all races loved each other. The greatest thing about it was people being together. I don't know whether they thought, "Well, the kids growing up together would be great," but it was. All those kids that grew up that way, wherever they are and their kids to follow, will be free of racial problems. Even with my mom, she didn't seem to have a bone of prejudice. I remember her saying they were all wonderful people. I could bring home Japanese or white kids for lunch and she'd say, "Well, you brought all your friends. Let's fix food for them."

Later I made sure my kids and grandkids were in integrated playgrounds. By the time they're grown, they won't be worried about meeting people of different races and going to places in Europe or anywhere. You begin to feel comfortable everywhere you go. So I think we happened to be in the right place at the right time. We could have been in a nicer-looking area, but I don't think it could have been more balanced, as far as all kinds of people sharing is concerned. I wish there was more of that going on now.

When I got into the professional end of music, the one problem I didn't have was getting along with different people. I always felt comfortable. Years later when Jerry Fielding hired me for the Groucho Marx show, *You Bet Your Life*, I was thrown in with fifteen white guys, and a couple of them asked me, "Well, do you feel a little strange? You're the only black in this band."

"No, it's great!"

I wasn't worried about that. I was happy to get a good job and was just trying to be the best musician. I wasn't like a lot of people, who get in this environment and say, "Well, they're white people. Do you think they like us or dislike us?" There's all this stuff sparking before you can be "Hey! How's everybody?" That little fear sometimes will come out, and I've seen it happen with people who didn't have this kind of upbringing.

A friend of mine, John Anderson, from Birmingham, Alabama, was once doing a big band job with me for Jerry Fielding. I'm the only black in the reed section and John's in the trumpet section. During the intermissions he'd hang on to me, because that way he felt comfortable. "Hey, man, I don't think they like me. They don't talk to me, and I just don't feel right." He was uncomfortable and I was having a ball! I told him that I was in the same situation he was and that everything was fine. The guys talked to me. In other words, nothing bothered me, so it didn't bother them. I fit in. If you're looking a little frightened and you're not socially prepared for something like that, of course, it's going to come off that way. He didn't last and you could see he wouldn't, because he was uncomfortable. I think it came from his early childhood, growing up in Birmingham, where there was a lot of friction between the races.

We also drew inspiration from the school, Jordan High School on 103rd near Alameda Street, studying with Joseph Louis Lippi and Verne Martin. That's definitely where I started music. Verne Martin came around 1940 and was actually more of a musician than Lippi, who was a versatile musician, though a jack of all trades. He played violin, enough trumpet to play better than the students, and could play the other instruments well enough to encourage everybody. But Verne was a fine saxophone and clarinet player. He was a part-time studio player, tall guy, about six-feet-six or so, and very thin. We liked him, because we could see there was another quality in his playing.

"Hey, you play studio jobs with that kind of sound?"

"Yeah, this is the sound that the studio players use."

So we were intrigued by that – Eddie Davis, Bobby McNeely and me. We hung together and rehearsed together. We said, "Maybe we should catch Martin to see if he'll stay after class and teach us what he's doing, because there's something about that sound that's great." He went for it.

"I'll stay. I'll bring a sandwich and teach you guys, and just go right to work from school."

And we'd ask him, "Why is your sound like that?"

"Well, one thing is, I'm using vibrato. We have to use vibrato to make the tone work, and help intonation."

Only a few teachers taught vibrato, but Mr. Martin would discuss it openly and show us how. He'd play with a straight tone and then start doing vibrato. We just looked at each other. We didn't know if we liked it or not, but it was different; it was interesting. We learned so much that first day with him. This guy was a master.

"When we're playing in the studio, we're matching vibratos; we're listening to the lead player; we're matching his sound."

And we thought about that. He was a nice man.

The faculty wasn't integrated. There weren't any black teachers then, but the teachers that wanted to come to that area had to be special people. For example, if you're a teacher and I'm your supervisor or principal, and I say, "This area's rough. There's a lot of black kids," or a lot of Mexicans or a mixture. "Do you want to go there?" You can bet that a lot of people said, "Let me go where I'm comfortable." So the ones that came out were very special people and we got beautiful human beings. They didn't come just for the money, because they had a long ride – no freeways then – and they knew they had to really teach. The teachers that we got were dedicated, and if you wanted to learn and ask questions, stick around. Both music teachers would say, "Hey, do you want to stay after? I'll teach you this, I'll show you that." And it paid off. That environment was very healthy for us.

Watts was very conducive to creativity. When Charles Mingus, Bobby and Cecil (Big Jay) McNeely, and I were going to school, we saw Simon Rodia working on the Watts Towers. Mingus lived on

108th Street, the McNeely brothers on 109th, and the Towers are on 107th. When we went to Mingus' house, we'd walk right by and see Rodia. Of course, then it was only a four or five foot wall, no towers yet. This was about 1935, 1936. We didn't know what it was. Sometimes as we passed by, he'd be working. We'd hassle him and he'd chase us away.

Simon Rodia was a little Italian guy with an old, dirty hat; a very quiet man, who didn't seem to have any friends and lived alone. Most of the neighbors ignored him and he didn't talk very much. I don't know if he spoke English. Although he was a full-grown man, it seemed that he weighed only about 100 pounds. He carried an old burlap sack on his back that he'd fill with little rocks, bottle caps, broken bottles, shells, and all that material he was gathering to build his towers. Mingus and I would take these gum machines and put them on the railroad tracks. When the Watts Red Cars would come by, they would break the cast iron bottoms, which held all the pennies, maybe five dollars worth, which was a big haul. There would be a lot of litter like that along the tracks, and Rodia would pick it up and make the most of it. Simon knew what he was doing with it, but we had no clue. Most people thought, "That crazy guy, what's he building?" We had never seen anything like that before, and he just kept adding to the structures. It wasn't until later that we could see that the guy was very artistic and knew where he was going.

So it was a great period and very productive. It seemed to be very rich in producing all kinds of talented people.

2
Musical beginnings

I always liked music, and there was always music in the house. We had a piano and mom and dad always played good records. We loved the Louis Armstrong band, Fletcher Henderson, Duke Ellington. Uncle Jimmy played piano a bit, and my mother liked to sing. My grandmother was very instrumental in keeping a lot of music around us. In fact, she started me on piano at ten and my sister at twelve.

"I want my grandchildren to come to my house on weekends, and I will pay for the lessons."

Every Friday night we'd go to my grandmother's. Saturday morning we'd be up bright and early. She would make sure we had breakfast and we'd have to do some housecleaning. She kept us busy. Piano lessons were about noon, which I didn't like. I was at an age when I thought I could do better things on Saturday, and I was the only boy at the lessons. I thought, "This is so boring." And I hated to practice! I love it now, but then boys weren't too happy about playing piano. Most people that you saw playing it, you weren't too impressed with them in any way.

Dad first brought a saxophone into the house. He noticed the way my mother and her friends loved the big bands and the musicians. Whenever Louis Armstrong, Duke Ellington, or another big band would come to town, everything stopped. My dad and his friends would go to the performances, and they noticed how the ladies liked those bands. Soon after, they went out and bought some instruments. They probably bought them hot, because dad loved to deal.

Dad started on saxophone, figuring he could master this quickly, as he did most things, whether it was fixing a car or plumbing. He taught himself to be a great plumber. So he figured he'd be in Duke's band right away, because it couldn't be hard for him. He took two or three saxophone lessons, but didn't seem to be getting anywhere. Dad responded by trying to blow harder. I was about ten and it never bothered me. But one day, while he was trying to play "When the Moon Comes Over the Mountain," Mrs. Craig, who lived next door, came over and said, "Mr. Collette, you'll never get the moon over the mountain the way you're blowing."

That's how my younger brother got a saxophone. But like my dad, Pat wasn't getting with it at all. He'd hide it somewhere, in the closet or under the bed, so nobody would find it.

For some reason the saxophone appealed to me. I thought, "Now, that would be a nice way to go. I'd have something to take to school and show off." That's how kids think. The next time I went for piano lessons, I had to wait for the proper time to talk with my grandmother. I let things settle down. The moment she relaxed and we were getting along, I said, "Grandmother, I'd like to stop piano."

"If you stop the piano, I'm not going to help you, because I know you'll be jumping from one instrument to another. I've been through that with my own children. They didn't stick with it. Now I'm having the same thing with you. I wanted you to be a great pianist. I wanted you to travel to Europe. Your music will take you all over the world, if you would learn it and be something. Now you're going to start jumping around."

She was so set on me being a classical pianist that we kind of fell out. I continued going to see her, but she didn't have the same warmth for me. We were no longer pals. Later she did follow my progress – she'd always check with my dad – and was pleased when it was clear that I was serious about music. About four years later I played a saxophone solo at her church and that cleared up the situation.

When I was about twelve and hadn't been playing saxophone for very long, my best friend, Vernon Slater, didn't play and I had to figure out a way to keep him close to me. So I taught him saxophone. At first we were both playing on mine. When our parents saw what we were doing, they got together and bought him one. So I started teaching when I was twelve, and all I could teach was what I knew, which at that time was one scale. But he got to be a great saxophone player.

I went to junior high school when I was around twelve or thirteen. They had an instrument class and I finally studied the saxophone. After I'd had the horn for about a year or so, I could toot and find certain notes. I was having fun with it, but after about six months at school I began to play. I learned pretty fast, my ears were good, and with all the music that my parents played, I began to get into it.

Bandleader at twelve

One night, when I was twelve, my parents went to a party at Dootsie Williams' house. He was a fine trumpeter, who had a big band then. That was pretty wild, a guy with a big band in our neighborhood. Sometimes I'd go by and hear them rehearsing. That was very fascinating to me, to see them drive up in their cars. They might have been only eighteen, nineteen years old, but we were twelve, so they looked like hotshots.

When I woke up the next morning, there was a big trunk full of music that Dootsie's band didn't need and that they'd given to my parents. I figured, "I've got to hear this stuff. The only way I'm going to hear it is if I've got a band." Not that I had to have a band, but I was really curious, as I would always be about something like that. So I got some of my friends – Vernon Slater on saxophone, Minor Robinson, a drummer, Charlie Martin on piano and Crosby Lewis, trumpet – and we started rehearsing the music. Kids will do it. When you get older, everything has to be just right. But kids will say, "An alto and a drum, we'll play." And that's what it's all about. It doesn't have to be perfect. You will learn more by getting together, than by playing alone. A lot of people say, "Practice, practice, and you'll be good." But there's a line that's stronger than that. When you start playing with one more person or two more, then it's interplay. You have to listen. That's the discovery period and we learned a lot of that early.

A little while later, when I was thirteen, we formed a band with Ralph and Raleigh Bledsoe, who were twin sons of one of the top doctors in the area, Ralph Bledsoe, Sr. They were a couple of years older than we were, but we were the local little guys in the area that were trying to be musicians. With their dad's help they found out who we were and we formed a band. The brothers played trombone and tuba. We had Minor Robinson on drums, Crosby Lewis on trumpet, Charles Martin on piano, and we had a tenor player, a Mexican guy named Gutierrez. We called him "Wimpy" Gutierrez. This was really a good band and we were anxious to go with them, because their dad could back them and we knew that this looked like serious stuff.

We didn't have any bookings except a party every now and then on a Saturday for three or four dollars. Fifty cents apiece wasn't bad payment at that time. But the doctor was a tough taskmaster, a disciplinarian, a big guy who never smiled, and his kids had to be doing it right. He just controlled everything. He'd come to rehearsal and we felt that pressure on us. We didn't like it and eventually fell out with them because of this. During a big meeting at the dad's office, he offered us twenty dollars for our book. It wasn't all the music that Dootsie had given me and twenty dollars wasn't too bad at the time. We could buy another twenty arrangements of what we wanted. So we took the money and said goodbye to those guys.

Shining shoes and exploring LA

As a kid I shined shoes with Vernon Slater. We knew each other before he started playing saxophone and we used to shine shoes all over downtown LA. I think that was one of the greatest experiences for a kid. We were eleven or twelve and we wanted to make some money, so we could buy suits for Easter. A suit cost fourteen or twenty dollars, and it would take us at least three weekends to make that money. If we made a dollar, a dollar and a half, that was a great day. Most of the shines were a dime; sometimes you'd get a quarter. That was a big tip. With a dollar ten in your pocket, that was a good day. We could have lunch for ten or fifteen cents, and could go to the show for five or ten cents. So that was big, big money. We were rich

15

for kids. We had made it ourselves; we were earning our own. I thought it was so great.

Shortly after that, when we became interested in music, that job helped us, because we found all the music stores, and we'd go hang in them and meet the people who would come in from the big bands: Duke's band, Artie Shaw's band or Benny Goodman's. Some of those guys would be in Lockie's Music Store in downtown LA, which was the big store for instruments and anything related to music. They'd be trying out horns and buying reeds. We'd stop in there every Saturday, and there were times we listened to Johnny Hodges or Harry Carney trying out a horn.

We didn't have any problems. Some of the white guys would kid us, because we were little black kids: "Hey, you think Joe Louis is going to win the fight? He can't beat the white guy." It was all this dialogue, but it didn't bother us. We'd just respond, "We bet Joe Louis wins," or something like that. It was the period when Joe Louis was coming up, and when he fought it was really a black and white war. Most times he was winning those battles and these guys would be sick. They'd be so angry that the black guy had won.

We found people who were not so friendly, but we also found some that were. There was one guy, Everett "Mac" McLaughlin, who had a shop and was one of the best repair guys you'd ever heard of. The shop was chaos; you couldn't find a thing. He'd be throwing screwdrivers here and hammers there. You had to walk over beer cans. We'd hang around and he'd fix our horns for nothing all the time. He'd put pads in and say, "Ah, don't worry about it." Mac was a genius. He and a guy named Bill Naujoks made a lower extension on the bass clarinet, so you could get four more lower notes. And they adjusted the fingering on the other side, end of the thumb key, with two or three buttons. They also made their own mouthpieces, which were the best.

There was George Tieck's Music Store. George and his brother Art were also great repair men. They'd look for us every Saturday. Most of the time we'd just hang there with them, spending maybe two or three hours in those stores. We were fascinated by the musicians, the mouthpieces, the horns – everything. We learned so much just being around the people who knew. They'd say, "Well, get a good teacher" or "Be sure you practice, and be sure you keep yourself straight." All those things were very important. We'd had a complete day by two o'clock and then we'd finally go home. Our parents never worried about us.

The Woodman brothers

An important inspiration for all of us in the Watts area was the Woodman brothers – Coney, William, Jr., also known as "Brother," Britt, and a little brother named George, who was a good dancer. They were only one to four years ahead of me, but they were playing jobs on a professional level when they were fourteen and fifteen. They were finished musicians. They worked three or four nights a week and were making pretty good money, maybe ten dollars a night. That was a lot of money in the mid-1930s, even for a whole band.

Their father, William Woodman, Sr., trained them all early and then sent them to very good teachers. He was a good trombone player, once offered the job with Duke Ellington's orchestra to play lead before Lawrence Brown, but refused because he wanted to stay with his kids. Thirty years later, Britt got the job that his father turned down. His dad knew: "They'll take my son, because he'll be good enough."

Brother played trumpet, alto sax and clarinet. Britt played trombone, clarinet and tenor sax. Then Coney played piano, guitar and banjo – "The Woodman Brothers Biggest Little Band in the World." They could get any combination of sound and could make all the music you could imagine. They had one hundred charts and arrangements that they knew from memory, as well as their own material, and they sang together. Joe Comfort was also in the band, playing bass and cornet, and he was amazing. He never practiced, but he'd pick up the trumpet and play. Tommy Dorsey's "Marie" was popular then. I think it was Paul Weston's arrangement, a beautiful arrangement. Joe would listen to the record and the next night he'd play it! He'd say, "I just heard it, picked up the horn and there it was." They also had George Reed and then Jessie Sailes on drums, and Jewell Grant on saxophone. I joined them when I was about fifteen. Whenever Jewell was away, they would use me in his place.

It was such a good band, man! And the experience of being around the Woodman brothers was so important because they were professional in their musical abilities and even in a lot of their attitudes. They set the stage for me becoming the kind of musician I had to be. I heard what musicians were supposed to do. It would have been different, if I hadn't heard that, and Brother also taught me clarinet.

They could be wild. We played all over, and once we were going down to San Diego. Brother was driving and trying to see how close he could come to the oncoming cars. "Watch me. I'm a real skilled driver," he'd say. Well, this time he scraped a car. We heard it. They had a '37 yellow Packard and we'd always be going ninety – I swear, *ninety*. Out on the road, trying to sideswipe cars, and going ninety. We were getting ready to get killed.

Britt always used to call me when he was with Duke Ellington. Once he said, "I'm kind of unhappy with my playing."

"What do you mean, Britt? What's going on?"

"Well, I don't seem to be any better than I used to be. I haven't improved in twenty or thirty years; I'm still playing the same thing."

I laughed. "If that's the case, then it just means a lot of us are catching up with you! You guys were so good, that you almost had the field to yourselves. Now it looks like you're not so much better than everybody; you're sort of where you're supposed to be."

When I laid that on him, he kind of chuckled. "Well, I can relax then."

"Just go ahead and have fun. You've been playing longer than all of us here."

Watts was known for the riots in 1965 and the Watts Towers. Mingus and I came from Watts, but the Woodman brothers were the strong points. They're even the inspiration for all of Central Avenue. What Mingus, me, Sonny Criss, the McNeely brothers, and others brought to Central Avenue came from them. The real credit goes to the Woodman brothers, who were doing it. We were all attempting to do it and were fortunate, the ones who lived in the Watts area, to hear them and be their friends and exchange ideas with them. In the Los Angeles part of Central Avenue people like Chico Hamilton, Jackie Kelson, Ernie Royal, and Dexter Gordon, had Samuel Browne, a great teacher at Jefferson High School, as their big influence. But ours was the Woodman brothers, because they not only could play individually, we would also see and hear them in a band with arrangements. So the Woodman brothers kicked it all off, and some of us picked it up from Watts and took it wherever.

3
Charles Mingus

A friendship

Before I was fourteen we broke up with the Bledsoes and I started my own band again. But now I needed a bass. Then I heard about Charles Mingus, who wasn't a bass player; he played cello. I kept hearing about this kid that lived on 108th Street: "You'll know him when you see him; he's bowlegged and he's always doing something different than anybody else." News traveled fast then. Somebody in town that was different, you would hear about it.

One day I was walking near Ninety-eighth and Compton, and I saw this bowlegged kid. His hair was shaved down the middle and he had a shoeshine box, but an unusual one, about three feet tall, that he carried on his shoulder.

"You've got to be Mingus, right?"

"How did you know?" He was so surprised.

"Well, I knew how you would look. Your legs . . . ." He didn't like that. "They also said you'd be doing something different. I shine shoes, and I know that my box would never be like that. What is that for?"

"I have my people sit up on the hood of a car, so I need a higher box."

That's what he was like. He would look at something and figure, "Well, heck, it could be different." Then everybody would say, "This guy must be nutty." But he'd be laughing, because he had figured something out. Back then some of those cars had fenders that were more of a seat, and people used to sit there. That was one of my dad's favorite little seats. So Mingus knew.

Then I said, "Look, I know you play cello, right?"

"Yeah, why?" He was not too happy to talk to me at this point.

"Well, if you've got a cello, I've got a band. I'm thinking about getting a bass player in there. If you can get rid of the cello and get a bass, you got a job." By then I was smart enough to know that I've got to have a bass to give us that other feel.

That's the first time I sparked him. He got so excited. "I'll ask my dad," and he took off. He didn't seem to be too thrilled with the cello. It seemed his parents were making him do it. There was a Mingus family trio with sisters Grace playing violin and Vivian on piano. Apparently, his parents wanted them to have a classical trio.

About two weeks later, he found me and said that his dad had gone to the music store and traded the cello for a bass. I said, "Well, I got a job on Saturday. You with me?" I didn't know whether he could play or not. The things he did that first Saturday night on the bass showed that he had real ability. It's amazing to hear somebody with musical talent. Looking back at all the players that I've met, you can hear from the beginning whether or not the individual is going to be a great talent. Some people will play well, but don't have that spark. Mingus' notes that first gig were not right – not that he didn't have good ears. It's just that he didn't know where the notes were and maybe his tuning was not perfect, but his time was good, if you could believe that, and he was plucking at the bass. All of a sudden there was a feeling and a choice of rhythm patterns right from the beginning that told me this was someone special.

Then he got serious. Charles hung around me a lot and he was always in my band. We'd practice all the time, going from house to house with bass and saxophone. Every morning in the summertime he was on my doorstep with his bass. He'd walk from 108th to Ninety-sixth Street with a bass on his back to jam before breakfast. Then we'd get on the Red Car at 103rd and Grandee, near the Watts Towers, and ride into Los Angeles for the half hour it took us to get there. As soon as we got on board, Mingus would unzip his bass cover and say, "C'mon, let's jam." People liked it; usually we played

21

some blues. It got so that whenever we were in the car, they expected us to play. It was very pleasant, especially with the rhythmic motion of the car, swaying as it went along. We also rehearsed with trombonist James Henry, who later became Chico Hamilton's brother-in-law. I hadn't met Chico yet.

Mingus also started feuding with the Bledsoe brothers. At that time there was a piece out called "Slap That Bass." The bass viol was just coming into its own, and there were still a lot of tubas in the bands. Whenever Mingus would see the Bledsoe brothers, especially the one that played the tuba, he'd say, "Slap that bass! Slap it! . . . but you can't slap a bass horn!" The guy was mad at him, but that's how his creative mind would be thinking.

We began to play dances at the Odd Fellows' Hall in Watts and other places. When I got a car, we'd drive up Central Avenue to a place called Finley's, where they had chili and malts and hot dogs. We'd play Jimmie Lunceford records there all the time and Mingus would just eat. That's when he started putting on all that weight. The band would even chip in to feed him to see how much he could eat. We always hung out in these spots to meet people and to listen to the music of the big bands, which is the way you got your schooling. Later, we got to see the Lunceford band at the Shrine Auditorium. The place was packed – five to six thousand people like sardines. We were right up against the bandstand. Forget the bathroom. You were right there for four hours.

The Lunceford band was our favorite then. The excitement, the arrangements, the feeling of closeness . . . not many other bands had that "family" feeling. They worked together so well, drew upon each other's talent. Willie Smith, Joe Thomas, Dan Grissom, Trummy Young, Gerald Wilson, Snooky Young, drummer Jimmy Crawford, arranger Sy Oliver. They had that vibrance, the feeling, the tempos. That band's pacing and togetherness in live performance just weren't equalled anywhere else. I loved Duke and Basie, but there was something different about Lunceford.

Mingus wrote about this period in his book *Beneath the Underdog*. We weren't quite as wild as he portrays; he was probably 50 percent accurate. Mingus was a very creative, very inventive guy, who loved a lot of fanfare, a lot of the "something was happening." As a young man he would always be doing something to attract a crowd or have people look at him. He was into his own thing, when it was very strange to do that. He shaved his head, was very heavy, and had bowed legs. So he kind of stood out and he wasn't a shy person at all; he could do things like that without feeling self-conscious. Every now and then he would pick fights with guys that he couldn't beat just to keep some activity going. He fought one guy about three times and finally beat him. He just wouldn't give up.

We were active young guys, but, heck, we were kind of nice young guys, meaning no drinking and dope at that time for us. We had an apartment and would have young ladies come by. But there was no way to pull any fancy stuff or get real serious with them, because I don't think we were aware of any kind of protection, maybe condoms a little bit, but it was almost hush-hush. If you had anything to do with any young ladies at, say, age fifteen or sixteen, you knew good and well that it would be marriage, shotgun-type, from the father. We all knew that was the word. You couldn't even sneak, because all of a sudden a guy would knock on your door and say, "All right, let's do it up." So we were very careful, because that's all we knew.

Mingus lived on 108th and Compton, and this apartment was on 103rd or 104th. We'd go by with Cokes and sandwiches and have a ball. Dope and the drinking wasn't there. I think when Mingus wrote his book, he wanted to put a little extra spice in there about those parties and having our own apartment. Actually, it wasn't really ours; it was my friend Amos Green's place. We could spend a couple of hours after school sometimes, if we wanted, but that wasn't every day. We were too serious with our music to spend all that time. Mingus let his fantasies carry him away. At one point he imagined having sex with many, many ladies in the same night and all that. I guess it was good reading for a lot of people.

Much of what he wrote about my dad was true. If you asked my father something, he would tell you his feelings. I was working the Follies by then with the Woodman brothers and Maxwell Davis. Mingus worked there with me a little later. He'd wait for the ladies after the show, hoping that one would wink at him. He'd fall in love every day, every week, and then there'd be another problem. He'd say, "Gosh, how could I really make this woman love me?" Mingus always had his problems with the ladies, trying to figure them out, especially at that period. He'd visit me almost every day during the summer, and we would jam a while. If my dad happened to be home, he'd catch him. Dad was always anxious to give some advice. "Let me tell you what you do." So I'm pretty sure all that stuff my dad told him was true. He might have elaborated on a few things, but my dad was ready to help you. He was definitely instrumental in trying to solve Mingus' love-life problems.

You never knew what Mingus was going to do. Once during the late 1940s, we were in Oakland, California, with Floyd Ray's big band. After the show was over, we were standing outside, talking, and Mingus suddenly just took off running and jumped on the hood of this brand new car. The hood caved in under his weight and the top went with it. The owner, who was out there, just about went crazy.

"What are you doing!?"

All Mingus said was that he felt like running over the car. It was just an impulse.

His music was that way too, and it was always interesting, not always the same. Tomorrow night he would start somewhere else and try something completely different. Even as a kid, that was his personality. He didn't come from any mold. When I was in the service, the letters he sent me wouldn't say, "Hello. How are you?" They'd begin, "You told me to practice eight hours a day and I'd be the best bass player. I'm doing that now and I can't get along with anybody. I'm playing better than everybody, and everybody's playing out of tune. I tell them to tune up and they want to fight me!"

I introduced Mingus to Red Callender, who was his first teacher. After I was hired for the band at the Million Dollar Theatre, I found out that the soundtrack for the film on the program had been done by great musicians, including Lee Young, Oscar Bradley and Red Callender. They knew the chorus girls at the Theatre and would come by two or three times a week to catch the show and see the girls.

I told Mingus to come and I'd introduce him to Red. I figured that Mingus would probably want to study with him and he did. They used to go to a theater on Central Avenue called the Rosebud after the lessons. Red would use the money from the lessons to pay for the movies. Then Charles studied with Herman Rheinshagen, one of the finest classical bass teachers. Mingus worked hard with rubber balls for about a year, just those rubber balls in the hand, because Rheinshagen's technique required powerful hands. So Mingus had strength, and when he'd start playing the bass, you'd hear something.

Mingus was very serious. When I got back to Los Angeles from the navy in 1946, he and his first wife, Jean, had two sons, Charles III and Eugene. Jean told me that Charles would get up around 8 a.m. and go straight to the bass in his pajamas. He'd play until noon, when he'd get a bowl of cereal and toast – something simple not to waste any time – and then continue playing until about 6 p.m. Then he'd switch to the piano, take a dinner break at nine o'clock, and return to the piano until two o'clock in the morning. That was his daily routine and Jean was ready to go out of her mind. She took care of the kids and the house, and Charles couldn't find his shoes. She was so beautiful that she got a job and waited while he got it together. Charles just had to play and he was also writing all day. He had all kinds of music scores. When you went to his house, there was music all over the floor. He complained to me that his back ached, because he sat over the piano for so long. That routine lasted for several years and the times were rough, but Mingus would just blot everything else out except for the music.

And it was always his music ... with one exception. We talked about Duke Ellington, kept feeding our coins into the jukebox machines, and listened to everything he did. Mingus never mentioned anyone else. He may have looked at some classical scores, but I never saw him doing it, and in the years we were together he never mentioned any other composers, such as Schoenberg. Even when he was studying with Red Callender and Rheinshagen, he never mentioned studying classical scores. He certainly studied the technique. But Mingus' sound was in his head, and it came out when he played the piano. The way he voiced on the piano and played it so well with his own style, it was uniquely his and the sound was within him. It didn't come from studying a Schoenberg score, for instance. Some people have a need to pin his music down. "Where'd he get that?" But there was no indication when I was around him that he was ever into anyone else's music in that way ... except Duke. Mingus was an original.

The Town Hall concert

I don't exactly know why, but we were closer than brothers. I used to say things to him and he would believe it, like nobody else could say anything different, and I would just tell him what I had heard. He would take that to be *the* word. He was a problem guy in a sense, but when I was around he was peaceful. There were times when he definitely needed me, because a lot of people didn't understand him. He'd get depressed and discouraged easily. He needed a good friend to keep his spirits high and that was me; I'd encourage him. When I'd come around, he was like a kitten – a nice, nice man. I don't know what started it, if it was because I was there to suggest that he get the bass, but he had all the faith in the world in me.

Charles and I fell out once, at the time of the Town Hall concert in New York in 1962. We didn't really fall out, but we screamed at each other. That had never happened in all those years, as wild as he was, and he would fight anybody at the drop of a hat. Preparing for the concert, he was giving everyone a bad time. The guy from United Artists Records called me up and said, "Mingus says he's got to have you here for this concert." They had thirty-five pieces, ten saxophones. No way in the world he needed me musically, but he did need me for moral support and whatever else I could give him. He told the guy, "I cannot do it unless Buddy's here."

I flew into New York just before the first rehearsal and took a cab to his place. I arrived just after he'd hit Jimmy Knepper in the mouth. When I walked in, the lamp was broken and music was all over the floor. The first rehearsal was at midnight.

I asked, "What happened with the lamp?"

"Man, Jimmy Knepper called me a name and I had to hit him."

They were so tight that no matter what Jimmy called him, it wouldn't have done that. They used to drive through the South with Mingus in the back and Jimmy, a white guy, up front driving and wearing a chauffeur's cap! They did all the tricks that you can imagine. They really loved each other and wrote a lot of music together. Mingus might have been under pressure, since the music wasn't ready.

"Man, we got a rehearsal now and I'm not finished. The copyists are waiting."

I didn't know what he was writing, but he had about thirty pieces with part of the melody finished, but no rhythm or piano. He said, "Start filling in, because we have to rehearse tonight." So I threw off the topcoat, got down on the floor, and started writing to fill in the parts. Mingus wrote in a peculiar way. I couldn't make out a lot of it, but I'd known him a long time and I could be as free as I wanted, doing all kinds of strange things.

"That looks great!"

The stranger I got, the happier he got.

"Man, you're really onto some new stuff!"

There was some weird stuff and when we got to rehearsal that night, some of the guys couldn't figure out the strange rhythm patterns. Mingus always worked like a madman, maybe taking a whole day to figure out how a particular pattern should be worked out. "How can I split triplets another way?" He could really use his mind experimentally.

At the rehearsal Jimmy Knepper came, missing one tooth, and they were again like lovers, man, they were so close. He couldn't play the trombone, but he still brought his music. He was dedicated to Mingus. We rehearsed from midnight until about three in the morning, because a lot of the musicians, like Snooky Young, Bernie Glow, Ernie Royal, Milt Hinton, and all the fine players, would be doing record dates until eleven o'clock. Each night, after rehearsal, Jerome Richardson and I would go across the street with Mingus to have breakfast, and each night he'd want to quit.

"I don't want to do the concert."

And I'd say, "Man, don't blow the concert. Do it."

"Well, okay then."

He could hear my voice. I don't know why, but that was the way it happened.

Town Hall was potentially a marvelous concert, which he spoiled because he was fighting with George Wein, the producer, who wanted to have a concert. Mingus wanted an open recording session, where you'd play a tune, then stop if you didn't like it and do it again. When the performance began, we all had tuxedos on and Mingus walked out in his blue jeans, short-sleeved shirt, leather vest and sandals with no socks. He went to the mike and said, "George Wein said this is going to be a concert, but it's not going to be a concert. It's going to be an open recording session. So if you don't like that, get your money and get out." Everybody laughed, thinking it was stand-up comedy, and they applauded. Mingus looked down, as if to say, "What's the matter with these people?"

So we went on. We'd play a piece and he'd stop it in the middle. Everybody got uptight, because we didn't know what was going on. He walked to the mike at one point and said, "I wouldn't like that, would you?" Then he went back to the orchestra and called another number. And this is a marvelous band, the best jazz players in New York. Trombones: Eddie Bert, Jimmy Cleveland, Britt Woodman. Reeds: Eric Dolphy, Pepper Adams, Jerome Richardson, Zoot Sims, Charles McPherson. Milt Hinton on bass. Trumpets: Snooky Young, Ernie Royal, Clark Terry. During the first set we didn't finish one number.

Finally, there was an intermission. We were so frustrated. He had marvelous music and we didn't play half of it. He had played games with all of us. It was a real tease and Mingus knew what he was doing. When somebody like George Wein would go against what he wanted, he would fight, even to the point of hurting himself.

Mingus' uncle, a clarinetist, came on with a Dixieland group after the intermission, and the audience loved it. Then we got on stage again and he was in the same mood. Time passed and he still wasn't playing anything, just stalling and doing nothing, and all the people sitting there. We were just dying by now, because what could we do?

He wasn't calling it. We couldn't just play his music with that size band. About eleven-fifteen, Mingus walked off stage like that was it and the stagehands began to slowly pull the curtain. Nothing was going on and they wanted to get out of there. It was a disaster until Clark Terry – he's a beauty – went into "In a Mellotone," which wasn't part of the program, and the band started jamming like you've never heard a band jam. The guys started setting riffs and the crowd ran and pulled the curtains back. You know, it's New York, man! It must have lasted about half an hour, and everybody soloed and jammed and set riffs. Mingus was completely surprised. I guess he couldn't get upset with the guys. Everybody was so hungry and pent up with emotions that we jumped on it. He finally came back and participated in the jam. So that was our big finale, which lasted about half an hour. That's what saved the concert.

It was good that I was there, because he wouldn't have done what little he did. We got 50 percent of him with me being there; if I hadn't been there, he could have killed that whole thing. Some time after the concert, we had a meeting at Britt Woodman's house. His wife Clara made dinner, and he wanted us to come over the next day so we could all be together, all of us from Watts. We began to talk.

Mingus said, "Buddy, man, you said that if I got the best guys that they could play my music and they would play it, read everything."

I said, "I think they did a very good job, because you have very difficult music."

"Well, I don't think they played it like they could have, because you said it would be perfect."

"Now, wait a minute." I had to cool him down. They were excellent players, who came and gave their time after midnight. No paid rehearsals. They'd come in after doing record dates, and they'd get parts written as high and hard as he could write. "Man, that's great when you get people that will come in and play your music, that will want to play music for you like this, and I think you got to give them more credit than that." He was still kind of unhappy. I said, "Would you do the same for them?"

"I don't play anybody's music but my own."

"You had the sounds in your head, and you're bringing thirty-five people together to be like Mingus. You don't do that in a couple of rehearsals." We didn't really fall out, but that was the heat of the thing.

Then Mingus said, "And I'm also unhappy with you, because you're not doing your own music."

"What do you mean I'm not doing my own music?"

"I'm the only one out of our group from Watts who is still writing his own music. You guys are all doing studio work. You sold out."

"I do studio work, but in the meantime I'm always doing my own music." Mingus didn't know that I'd been writing and had kept my quintet.

Then he finally loosened up and got warm. "I thought you had turned on us, and you were just doing studio work, and you didn't want to do your own stuff." Of course, he didn't like studio work very much and in his way he was right.

Before leaving New York after the Town Hall Concert, I went to visit my friends Dee and Mario, who lived in Greenwich Village. Mingus and I took a cab, and when we got there I realized it was right across the street from the Ninth Circle, a hangout for musicians, actors and writers. Mingus loved it and wanted to go in. I asked him to first meet my friends, who I hadn't seen in ten years or more. After maybe five minutes, he said he had to go, that people were waiting for him.

Dee, Mario and I were drinking wine and talking about Los Angeles and friends. About forty-five minutes later the bell rang and there was Mingus.

"You know what happened to me? When I ran out of here, I got hit by a car and I've been to the hospital and checked out. I'm OK. The guy who hit me was a doctor and here's his card."

My friends were looking pretty sceptical, but I thought he must have been telling the truth, maybe with some exaggeration. He always had unusual things happen to him, ever since he was a kid. He was still anxious to get to the Ninth Circle, so I told him I'd be over in half an hour. Of course, as these things go, after forty minutes I'm still there and Mingus is at the door again.

"Hey, you gotta come over with me this time." He was very

excited, like there was real trouble over there. "This guy was calling me names and I cut his tie off. I had my knife. I took it out and cut it off. I told him that you were my psychiatrist and I was going to bring you over so you can tell him that I'm not well."

I looked at my friends. "I got to go this time." We said goodbye and they wished me well. We crossed the street, went inside the club, and there was this crowd of people waiting for Mingus' psychiatrist. I go right up to the guy with the cut shirt; a whole circle of it was missing, and he was kind of laughing.

"I don't understand. I always call him names and we kid around, but this time he got mad at me."

"Look, I'm his psychiatrist. He's been upset by many things. His wife's pregnant. He's been under a lot of pressure getting ready for a recent performance." The crowd is all around us listening to my explanation. Suddenly everybody cooled down and Mingus was fine. He was so proud of my explanation. Hours later, we closed down the Ninth Circle.

When I returned to New York in 1963 to conduct for Ella Fitzgerald, I found out that Jimmy Knepper had sued Mingus for hitting him in the mouth and the court session was about to take place. Jerome Richardson was supposed to be a character witness for Mingus, but he said he had some work and asked me to take his place. I didn't see that I had much choice, so I joined Britt Woodman as Charles' character witnesses. The case was heard by three judges and Mingus' lawyer was very dramatic, a lot of show biz. He got a lot of emotion into his presentation, talked about Mingus' wife being pregnant and the pressure he was under. Whenever the judges tried to ask Mingus a question, he would take the answer wherever he wanted. Finally, one of the judges asked the lawyer what was wrong with his client. And, again, we'd hear about the pregnant wife in the lobby and the pressure on Mingus. They were stalling.

Finally, they got to me and I had to walk a fine line. Jimmy probably figured we wouldn't go against him, but I was there to testify for Charles. I knew Mingus probably hit him; he'd told me that when I arrived at his apartment that night. But they didn't ask me that question. They asked me if in the years I'd known Charles,

I'd ever seen him hit anybody. I told them I'd never seen him hit anyone, and that was the truth. I'm pretty sure he had, but I hadn't seen it. I explained that to Jimmy. He's cool.

I don't know how the suit was resolved, because I was back in Los Angeles shortly afterward. It was not a pleasant situation. Yeah, thanks a lot, Jerome!

Jazz at Monterey

When we were kids – eighteen or so – Mingus and I would test each other. He would write the first part of an arrangement or a piece, then I would finish it. Our game was to see if people could tell where one stopped and the other started. We could do that because I knew what he did – his use of intervals and the way his pieces moved – and he knew me very well – my melodic orientation. We didn't write alike, because we were different, but that was the kind of thing we had going. Right from the beginning we wrote and part of it was bouncing off each other, writing and doing our own music, because we were inspired by Ellington and Billy Strayhorn.

When we first started going out to Central Avenue, where the bands were playing, and to Finley's and the 54th St. Drugstore, where they had jukeboxes with all the latest records, we would put money in to hear things like "Jack the Bear" by Duke Ellington, featuring Jimmy Blanton on bass. He inspired Mingus. We just played that over and over again. All of a sudden Mingus could play things like "Jack the Bear," because that's where his heart went.

We got a chance to be around Jimmy at the jam sessions after *Jump for Joy*, which was downtown at the Mayan Theatre, and featured Duke Ellington's band. After the show Jimmy, Ben Webster, and a bunch of the guys would go to sessions at places along Central Avenue like Honey Murphy's and Ivie's Chicken Shack. The guys would tell us where everyone was going after the show each night, and we'd be there. Blanton would come in, put the bass in a corner, and have a little food. Within an hour or so, Art Tatum or someone would sit down at the piano and the music would start. Ben was taking Jimmy to all the jam sessions, when Jimmy got sick with tuberculosis. Jimmy was getting thin, but he kept hanging in there and probably should have been getting some help. Ben cried like a baby after he died, because he didn't know Jimmy was sick.

Like Blanton, Mingus was never just a supporting bass player. He believed in creativity, in expressing his own side of everything. He knew music didn't have to be the same. You just never knew what he was going to do.

Mingus was so unpredictable and sometimes he used that to fire up his bands. We played together at the Monterey Jazz Festival in 1964. I helped bring some guys from Los Angeles to fill out bands for Mingus and Thelonious Monk. We brought Bobby Bryant, Red Callender, Melvin Moore, Lou Blackburn, and Jack Nimitz. Mingus had his guys with him: Charles McPherson, Lonnie Hillyer, Jaki Byard, Dannie Richmond. John Handy was also with us. That's when we did the *Mingus at Monterey* album.

Knowing how Mingus rehearsed and his style of music, the way he would change things on the spot, we should have had maybe one or two rehearsals, but we must have had about four. We all thought we'd catch other performances, but he had us rehearsing, fooling around, going over this, not using that. That was his system. He just kept trying things.

He and drummer Earl Palmer eventually got into it. We had a jam session one night with Mingus sitting in. It was the first time he'd ever played with Earl, and he didn't like the beat Earl was playing. "Man, he's rough!" I could see they weren't playing together at all. Afterwards, we all had dinner at a big restaurant and they were looking at each other.

Then Mingus asked, "You beat your wife, Earl?"

"What do you mean?!"

"You're rough on those drums, and if you're rough, I figured you're probably beating on your wife."

"What do you mean, man?!"

I told everyone to cool it. That was the way Mingus was psyching Earl out to get that extra charge from him on the bandstand.

The rehearsals went right up to performance time with Mingus changing the material. We didn't know what would happen. When we got on the stage, Mingus did nothing as we rehearsed. He probably knew what he was going to do, or didn't know exactly, but at least he'd tried everybody at the rehearsals and heard all these different things. He knew what he had, so he could pull it in any time he wanted a certain flavor. It was all, "Watch me." He started playing and then looked at me. I'd known him so long that I knew it meant "Do something." So I picked up my flute, walked to the front, and we just started talking to each other through our instruments. Everything was just so impromptu; the other musicians were on the edges of their chairs. The spontaneity was just amazing. You could not rehearse that to get it to where we had it. It was one of those amazing moments in life.

We had great people, who put their thoughts, feelings and talents together. Despite everything, there was love in that group ... and we had plenty of everything. Bobby Bryant was on trumpet, but Mingus and Bobby also didn't get along, partly because they were kind of alike. Bobby wasn't quite like Mingus, but they were robust, big guys. The looks they gave each other said, "I don't like you too much." You could see that whenever they were together. When Bobby tried to play his solo, Mingus said, "No, I'll let you know when." He just kept doing, "Down, boy." He did that with Bobby in the rehearsals and then during the concert. Bobby finally resolved, "Heck, I'm here. I'll just make the gig and go home."

When we did "Meditations on Integration," everyone was getting into it, playing solos. Mingus had two other trumpet players, Lonnie Hillyer and Melvin Moore, and he let them play. Bobby knew he wasn't going to get a chance. It was getting louder, more intense, really screaming. Then Mingus looked at Bobby and said, "Now!" Bobby at this point was so angry he hadn't played that he took his horn and blew the bell off it to show Mingus what he could do. And that did it. Mingus got the climax he wanted and the people just went crazy. As with Earl, he had psyched Bobby out. He knew Bobby was strong as a bull and he wanted a killer punch. Melvin and Lonnie played beautiful, but Bobby was like Gabriel's trumpet with power to spare. He blew like he was in the biggest band ever and that trumpet was topping everything. Finally, four thousand people just leaped into the air and screamed for about four minutes. Al McKibbon, a fine bass player, who was standing there, said, "I don't know what y'all did, but you sure did it."

There it was. Mingus had captured all these moods. He knew how to get them. He was like a little tease: "Not yet" or "Maybe you won't get any" and then "Okay, now!" It does work. It's what coaches do for fighters. Sometimes you need that little kick.

Life with Mingus

Most of the time it was a disaster to have Mingus around. I loved him, but he was worse than a child. He could cook, but he didn't know how to clean up after himself. The eggs would be on the floor and the ceiling. He couldn't find his shoes when he had to go to work, didn't have a white shirt, couldn't write a check. All he could really do was play the bass and piano, and write music. If he was around today he'd be rehearsing his group or doing something musical. He wasn't one to sit in the park for two or three hours in the afternoon. We'd go to a movie together and he'd say, "I'll be out in the lobby. I'm just too nervous." He was always thinking.

He came out here once to spend a few weeks with me. I picked him up at the airport. He came in with no money, just a couple of checks that he couldn't cash, because they were New York checks. That's when he'd first started dating Sue, who was his wife when he died, and he was on the phone three or four times a day with her for about half an hour each call. My phone bill was about $400 that month and I had to feed him. He wasn't like a guy that was down and out. He just didn't think about bringing money and he had no car. I'd come home at three in the morning after a late call and he'd say, "Buddy, come on. I want you to hear this tune." And I had to get up at five to get the kids ready for school. It was the longest two weeks. I was dying.

I took him to a couple of record dates. He was miserable there, because he kept thinking we were phrasing like studio players, very corny. And he was right, if you want to look at it like that, but that's what it was. Studio playing was very regimented; everything was dissected and scripted to the point that it was so stiff. It didn't swing and Mingus couldn't stand that.

"I can't stay here! You guys are phrasing terrible!"

He told this to everybody. That's the kind of guy he was. He believed in creativity; he believed in expressing his own side and letting everyone know.

Some years later Mingus was out here to play at Shelly's Manne Hole in Hollywood. During that time Gerald Wilson had a radio show, *Portraits in Jazz*, and Pat Willard, then a local writer, arranged for him to be on it. I remember tuning in the program, and I also remember thinking, "I hope this works," because they never really thought very much of each other's music.

Gerald welcomed Charles, saying he was glad to have him on the show, that he'd always loved his music.

Mingus said, "You've never liked my music!"

That was the beginning of an hour program that was filled with suspense and tension. There were dull, quiet moments when neither of them said anything. Gerald tried his best, but Mingus always had a comment that kept up the tension. At one point Gerald asked what he was doing in town.

"I'm here at Shelly's Manne Hole, but you're not going to come and see me," Mingus replied.

It was Gerald's worst nightmare. Mingus could be really cold and rough, always saying just what was on his mind, what he felt.

Afterwards, I called Pat Willard and suggested they try it again the next week, but include some of Mingus' old friends. Britt Woodman was living in town then, as was Red Callender, who Mingus loved. I told her I'd come on the show also. We'd talk about happier times; it would be a great show. And it was. We gave Charles a comfortable setting, talking about how we met, worked together, and the early years. It was night and day from the first broadcast.

I could do a whole book on him. People know certain stories about him, like that Jimmy Knepper story. Those are the ones that get around. But there was another side to him, a very quiet and a very nice side that he didn't show very much, unless he was in a comfortable setting. I would help him find that. Nothing that I did particularly. I was some person that he could be comfortable with and he believed what I said.

The final illness

Charles became ill with Lou Gherig's disease (ALS – Amyotrophic Lateral Sclerosis) in the mid-1970s. In the beginning it seemed that there was a period when he began to slow down. He was out here around 1976, 1977 to play at Shelly's Manne Hole in Hollywood, and I went over to see him. We'd always run and grab each other, and he tried to run but couldn't. It was almost like his body wouldn't move. I still ran over and grabbed him, but he was shocked that he couldn't do it. I hugged him, but the feeling was very strange. His skin felt like Jello, instead of the firmness you'd expect. I guess it was the deterioration of the muscles. I knew there was something wrong, but it seemed to come and go, and every now and then he'd feel better.

A little later I saw him in Tucson. I went there to do something with the Flute Club, and I knew he was there. So I went over to see him at the Doubletree Inn, where he was playing, and the flesh was still that way, though he could play a little. I just knew he was going through a lot. Every once in a while he'd say his back hurt, his foot hurt, things like that, but he was getting worse. He'd call me, but after a while that was hard. Sue told me that he had good and bad days. This was about a year before he died and Sue was still sending him out on jobs. He'd get top money, $10,000 a performance, but he wasn't playing well. Maybe he shouldn't have been doing it.

Near the end they moved to Cuernavaca, outside of Mexico City, and I didn't hear much from them. We were all wondering, "Is Charles going to make it or not?" Then one day I got a call from him. He didn't say very much, but I could tell that it was one of those calls: "If you're going to come, you'd better come. I've got to see you." I told him I'd be there. It was so short and abrupt; I didn't want any conversation. There was no need to say, "Well, what do you mean?" It was as clear as it had to be.

Charles and Sue met me at the airport in Mexico City. They came in a van from about seventy miles away. He was strapped in with the wheelchair and they had it chained to prevent it from rolling. Although he couldn't move his arms, his eyes and face lit up. We drove back over seventy miles of hills and winding roads to this place they'd leased that looked like a castle.

I was there only a couple of days, which was long enough. All I could do was sit and watch him. I could talk; he couldn't talk back. He'd be trying to, but it was painful. He'd show me his hands – he could move them a little bit – and his eyes said, "I'm going to play again." And I'd say, "Yeah, you'll play. We're going to do some stuff together this time." He always wanted to do that. His big wish was that I'd come to New York, because he figured they would know me better.

The day I arrived, folk singer Joni Mitchell had been there for a week. She left either that morning or the day before. She was there mainly to write lyrics to his tunes. He couldn't say yes or no, so he'd make a noise, "Aaahhh!," if he didn't like it. If it was something he liked, he would smile. It would have been nice to have been there with her. At least we would have gotten a chance to know each other.

His son, Eugene, and Sue were there, and they had a nurse from Mexico. They were sort of going out of their minds and seemed to think, "If we can just keep feeding him, he's going to get better." They were stuffing him with Mexican food – tamales and tacos and beans – and he could hardly eat it; it was running down his chin. No one was getting any sleep and desperation seemed to have set in.

They were going to this local lady, who was a healer, and had him eating two dozen snails a day. The snails were kept in one of the bathrooms and were all over the walls, everywhere. They were also out chasing cows in the fields, picking up the cow dung while it was fresh and hot, and putting that on his back over a recent scar. At one period the healer had to cut his back for something. But it was amazing. They showed me his back and eventually there was no mark there. I thought they knew what they were talking about, but it was desperation. People will do anything at this point.

It was lonely, because Sue and the others were crazy by this time. They had to be with what they were going through. I just sat; I didn't want to do anything. That's all he could do, so I became a part of it. Then came the classic line. It will always stay with me. He knew that I was busy, and that I couldn't stay forever. Mingus got up close, looked me in the eye and said, "When do you have to go?" I could tell every word he said was painful. I told him I'd have to leave on Saturday, which was the next day. I thought by saying Saturday, rather than tomorrow, it might seem further away. "Don't worry" – he looked so sad when I said that – "I'll come back." Then the tears streamed down from his eyes and I saw a little kid, just like a flashback. There he was, this little kid, who wondered about playing the bass. As the tears came down, he said, "Don't come back. Take me with you."

I went in the house to find Sue, and said, "You've got to bring him home."

"But we've got another six months' lease on the place."

"You guys are going crazy here trying to help him. Come to LA. I know you and Grace haven't been getting along, but everybody wants to help at this point. You can't do it all by yourself. We can all take him a few days. That's the only way to do it."

"Well, we'll think about it."

"Sue, I know him so well; you know I do. If he was home, that would mean a lot to him."

We didn't talk about it anymore, because it was painful for her. The next day she didn't think he wanted to go back to LA, because he wasn't feeling too good. So they took me back to the airport. Charles wanted to come along. It was a job. He was heavy, and we had to get him in the wheelchair and then up the ramp. We got to the airport, embraced, and I said, "Look, you're going to come home, I'm pretty sure. I talked to Sue." He kind of nodded like he was hoping that would work out. And I waved. When I left there, I was just done in.

One week later Sue called and I never heard her sound like that, not happy, but at least she was upbeat. She said they were coming home. I called his sister and everyone, and we started getting ready. But he didn't make it. They called back in about three days. He had died.

We had a great tribute here for him. So many people played. Charles McPherson, Jimmy and Jeannie Cheatham. I had a band. We did some of his tunes. Llew Matthews, Kenny Burrell, Frank Morgan, and Benny Powell all played, all day long. His body was cremated. He wanted Sue to toss the ashes in the Ganges River. And that was it.

4
Central Avenue

The scene

In 1938, 1939, we were old enough to hang out until three, four in the morning on Central Avenue, and it was a fun place. It was different then than it was in the forties. When I came back after being in the service, there was a big change, between 1938 and 1946. But in the thirties there was the excitement of the after-hours spots and the drugstores that had the malts and food late at night, where people could meet after whatever job they had. The 54th St. Drugstore was probably the prime place after hours. It was a big spot; they had all kinds of food there. The celebrities were out at night and anybody you wanted to see would be there. If the Ellington or Basie bands, or a big fighter like Jack Johnson, who was heavyweight champion of the world, were around on a Friday or Saturday night, they'd probably be hanging in there. It was great because you could mingle with them. You knew they were real people, which was always important for a young player. We heard people on records and they're standing right there!

Finley's, where we first hung out, was much smaller than the Drugstore, which had the space and the atmosphere for just hanging out. There was also a place called Brooks Bathhouse, if you wanted to go have a steam bath, get doused by buckets of water. It was run by Dudley Brooks' dad. Dudley was a pianist and a fine arranger. There were places like the Club Alabam on Central, near Forty-second Street, and the Bal Tabrin in Gardena that hired lots of chorus girls. And they were all very flashy women; all so beautiful and probably only about twenty years old then.

They had great soul food places, where they really knew how to fix a chicken and great peach cobbler, and the price was reasonable. For a dollar you could have a dinner, maybe cheaper than that in most cases. You would see a lot of guys going into the barbershops, especially on weekends, and getting their hair conked. It might have cost you a couple of bucks and you had to spend an hour or so to do that. But it was all part of getting ready for the night scene, being sharp. Sometimes they didn't have a lot of money, but they looked great. Even if it was your last two dollars, you got your clothes to the cleaners. The emphasis was on a little flash or even a new car. Maybe your house wasn't in great shape, but you had to hit the Avenue with your hat on and your new pinstripe suit. Everyone was anticipating what would happen at night. There was always going to be good jazz, there were always ladies dressed great, and that was the place to be.

There were these great dancers, The Three Rockets, and they were the sharpest three guys you've ever seen – tall and handsome. Most of the time they didn't have any money, but you'd never see it in the way they looked. Their suits were tailor-made, and they'd be borrowing two dollars or three dollars from you to get the shirts out of the laundry for that night. They knew sharp was it. Somehow that was much better than being ragged with a lot of money in your pocket. They used to jump on me about dressing. I wasn't ragged or anything, but I wasn't getting my suits tailored at the time. They called me "Baby Boy" and said, "We got to take you to our man and get you a suit." Those were my first suits, and they were great. Boy, I was sharp, and that was the scene.

The Avenue was a fun place. There was a lot of variety. There were even people who were playing pimp roles. Guys would be walking the street and chasing the ladies down and trying to get into that kind of activity. The pool halls were jumping, and there was gambling.

Most people worked, could pay the rent, and afford one or two nights on the town every week. Maybe twenty-five bucks a week was one of the top salaries. Most black people didn't have good jobs. There was no post office work then. There were only a few doctors to speak of, such as Dexter Gordon's father and Dr. Ralph Bledsoe, Sr. My mom would take occasional jobs like cleaning house or keeping the kids of some family out in Glendale or Beverly Hills. That wasn't much money. You might work all day for three dollars or five dollars.

My grandmother used to tell stories about Booker T. Washington and a few greats. You'd hear about this one person; you would try to relate to that, but it would be difficult when you saw your friends and all the people in your neighborhood. The guy next door to our house was a junk man, Mr. Craig. He would go out, get junk and sell it. That didn't appeal to me, but he did all right. At least he fed his family; he had about six or eight kids. But it was tough stuff: the little junk truck and he was dirty, and he was really working hard.

So when we started seeing the other world, meeting musicians, that was what was interesting. They were dressed nicely and it seemed they were enjoying themselves. There was a whole other magical thing going on.

Becoming a professional

I was still getting occasional gigs at the Follies Theatre downtown on Main Street. When someone would get sick, leave for a while, or go on vacation, I'd get a call to fill in for a week or so, however long they needed me. Mickey Rooney's father, Joe Yule, was one of the top comedians there. That was a tough job, especially with the ladies up on the stage – Tempest Storm, Lily St. Cyr – you could not believe. You're trying to read the part and . . . . Well, I was about fifteen years old. I wasn't even out of school.

It finally hit me in the eleventh or twelfth grade, after I'd done the Follies job a few times and was having some fun, what it was that I wanted to be. But I didn't know if I could make a living at it. Nobody had explained it to me. It dawned on me when all the kids in our class were asked, "What are you going to be when you graduate?" I said that I'd probably be a musician, but it shocked me, because I didn't really know that much.

Then I met some of the Jefferson High School guys in a battle of the bands at the Million Dollar Theatre in downtown Los Angeles. This competition was for a job in an all-black show with Lawrence

43

Criner and Nina Mae McKinney. They held an audition to see what band would get the job of playing for the chorus girls. I had my band with Mingus, Crosby Lewis, Minor Robinson, and the whole gang. The other band had Chico Hamilton, Jackie Kelson, and Al Adams on bass. Our band lost, which we were kind of ill about. We were about eighteen, upset, and Mingus was saying, "Oh, man, we lost this good job." We always wanted to get out of Watts to play. Then their leader, a Mr. Myart, came over and asked me to join their band. So I got a chance to do my first big show. We were making twenty-one dollars a week, a lot of money for a kid at the time. We could buy shoes; we could eat every day; and we still had five or six dollars left before we got our next paycheck. It was unbelievable!

It was a real growing period, a period of learning. We asked ourselves, "Is this what we really want?" And of course it was. We could see higher levels than where we were, and we met and enjoyed so many people, like Red Callender, Lee Young, Oscar Bradley, and Red Mack – the older musicians who'd come and listen to us. They had nice cars and some of them had nice homes. But the homes weren't the things that they are now with people. Home was just a place to be. Most of the time you were out eating or in the car. And that was Los Angeles in the late thirties, especially on Central Avenue. You might have a little apartment, some place to sleep and change your clothes, but you'd head out right away. Wash the car; go get it shined up or something. It was all flair; it really was. A lot of people weren't working, but they knew how to parlay that into some extra money somewhere.

After we left the Million Dollar Theatre, Al Adams organized his band with Chico, Jackie and me, Eddie Taylor, James Nelson and Lady Will Carr, who was a fine pianist. She could play anything with such speed. When she played, the audience just stopped. She had such great talent. Then we finally got Mingus on bass and Al stood out in front. He was a bass player, but he was no bass player like Mingus. We did a lot of jobs at the Elks Hall, which was on Fortieth Street and Central. The Elks held all the big dances, the big club affairs, where you'd hear people like T-Bone Walker or Lowell Fulson.

We once had a battle of the bands with George Brown's orchestra at the Elks. They were a good band of professionals, older than us, who played most of the social, black tie dances. We didn't think they were that great, because we had a pretty wild band with Chico, Jack, Mingus, and we could jam. We even had Illinois Jacquet with us one night and that was the first time he ever played tenor sax. He blew the bell off that horn. We first met Illinois and his brother Russell at the Ross Snyder Playground on Forty-first Street near Long Beach Boulevard, where a number of bands rehearsed. They might have been in LA six months before one of our tenor players, Eddie Taylor, brought them to a rehearsal. They jammed with us and played so well that when we lost our other tenor player, James Nelson, for that night, we asked Illinois if he would get a tenor. He liked it, and again played so well I guess he never forgot it. But he forgot the story. A few years ago there was an article in the *Los Angeles Times* that quoted him saying Lionel Hampton got him a tenor, when he joined Hamp's band. When I saw him, I said, "You know the first time you played tenor was – ." He said, "Oh, I forgot." It was only one night and he probably rented a tenor. Maybe a year later he went with Lionel Hampton and brought in a tenor, because he was playing alto when we met.

We won that band battle and we were an exciting band. We were listening to Jimmie Lunceford and I wrote some Lunceford-type pieces. George Brown and his guys hadn't heard us before. They were more conservative, and we were young and drawing from Basie, Lunceford and Ellington. I was copying their stuff off the records for the band and some of their tough pieces. We weren't supposed to be playing arrangements that tough, but we were rehearsing almost every night, could read very well, and we could jam.

We had some contact with Dexter Gordon then, but not much because he was like a fun guy, seemed to be all tongue in cheek, just laughter. He was a player and he knew where he wanted to go. Later, he finally got to be real serious. I heard that Sam Browne at Jefferson High School used to keep him after school and tried to make him play scales. He was not an easy guy to teach. We all kind of laughed at him. He was a big, tall guy, and he wore Li'l Abner-type shoes. His pants were way above the shoes, and there he was with this alto doing many gestures, while he played these amusing solos. Sometimes he'd take his horn out in the street, just on the sidewalk there, and start playing and kicking his legs out. He was kind of a character, but he could play and he made it with style.

Dex never played with us in the band, but he was jamming in the sessions of that period. He wasn't the kind of reader that Kelson and I were. We loved to read and worked with a guy named Snake White, who wrote such hard arrangements that everyone thought he was nuts. We'd seek out people with books because we wanted to be great readers. So we were in different circles than Dex. He was a soloist with a rhythm section, playing in different groups. Whereas with Chico Hamilton, who wasn't a great reader either, but he could read, we were into bands that had music that was written for us. Those players could only be hired for a certain job, maybe one calling for a tenor player who knows "Dinah" or "Sweet Sue." Dex was more into that and he was very creative with his solos.

Lloyd Reese

There were studious gangs among us, going back to the Woodman brothers, who all studied either with their dad, or their dad made sure they were with a good teacher. No one just decided to be a musician and then it happened. We had the fundamentals. A bunch of us, who went to Lloyd Reese and some to Sam Browne, had a more schooled kind of approach to the music. You'd analyze it, figure it out, or write the arrangement, make sure the chords are right, and play in tune. There were certain basics. But there were also a lot of other musicians, who did not adhere to those concepts very much and just said, "Look, I'm playing good" or "I got the solo off the record and I know I'm good." They never really got the basics from a teacher, which doesn't mean they didn't sound good.

About 1940, I started studying with Lloyd Reese, who had played alto sax and trumpet with the Les Hite band. A lot of us did. I knew Lloyd was teaching and the word was out: here was a good teacher. I

46

didn't know what this kind of teacher would mean to me, except he sounded interesting.

There were two guys that I sent to him first as a test case, my two buddies: Bobby McNeely (Big Jay's brother) and Eddie Davis – not Lockjaw Davis. We all went to school at Jordan, but I was a little better than they were at the time. So I figured that if I see these guys improving, I'll know that I've got to get in there. Well, they came back, man, and they were working on tunes and they were working on reading and they had the piano going. After a couple of months, I called up Lloyd Reese.

He said, "You're a friend of Bobby and Eddie. They told me that I'd meet you."

"Yeah. When can we start?"

"Well, we thought you'd better come in. We got the guys doing pretty well now."

That's why I got with Lloyd Reese, and we hit it off real well.

He taught in his home on Jefferson Boulevard near Maple. All of his students had to play piano, which I thought was good, because then all the students had a pretty good foundation for whatever they wanted to do. You'd also be reading better; you'd be blowing all your tunes; you could transpose. He was covering everything. Most of us could write, most could conduct. You were getting all that other knowledge; he was not just grilling you on technique. Most other teachers were just: "I'll give you this book and I'll give you that book, and then you go out to play." This guy was preparing you to be a giant. He was opening our minds to being very musical.

Lloyd could not only teach the writing and good habits, but he would also pick up a horn. He hadn't played alto in a few years, when I met him. But whenever someone was having trouble with harmonics, he'd say, "Let me see your horn and your mouthpiece." And he'd just go on up to the top of the horn, almost like a doctor. "Oh, really? I'll take care of that right now."

He took up the trumpet when he worked with Les Hite at Frank Sebastian's Cotton Club in Culver City. They brought in an arrangement and the trumpet players complained about how hard the parts were. He listened and said, "Couldn't be that hard." He had a frame of mind, where he wouldn't allow that. One guy said to him, "The trumpet is harder than the saxophone." So he secretly went out and bought one, got the books, learned the positions, did the long tones, intervals, going one step at a time. Within a year or so he could play second or third trumpet. That amazed the guys and his solo playing on the trumpet was something else. I think with his versatility, that sort of opened up some versatility in our minds.

One day Phil Moore, Sr. – a wonderful pianist, teacher, vocal coach, bandleader, arranger – and Lloyd had a showdown at the black musicians' union on Central Avenue. I wasn't there, but I heard about it. They liked each other and were friendly rivals, pretending that one knew more than the other. Phil Moore was a brilliant man, but Lloyd was a real scientist. He could always hear something to be improved upon, even in the best musicians. He'd say, "Ben Webster came by yesterday and he was stumbling over this same thing," letting you know that even the greatest musicians were still human. So Lloyd and Phil had a trumpet and piano competition at the union with about fifteen or twenty people present. They chose "Stompin' at the Savoy," and agreed to play the first eight bars in the original key of D flat, then going up half steps every eight bars until somebody fell out – D flat, then D, and so on. You've got the bridge in the key of E flat, then E. They went on for about a chorus and a half before Phil Moore dropped out. Lloyd was still playing the changes for another chorus.

He also had a workshop rehearsal band once a week and all of his students were in it. It was the most marvelous experience we'd ever been through. Lloyd would have us get out a certain arrangement and we'd play it. "Okay, let me hear the saxes give me a B-flat chord," and we'd all hit a B-flat chord. "Second tenor push in a little bit and third tenor pull out. Baritone, let me hear you again. Yeah, you're a little flat, too." He might have taken five minutes or so on that, hitting the B-flat chord. Then he might have asked us to hit another chord, just to hear whether he was fooled on the B-flat chord. "Well, now, you guys are not listening." The whole band would be just sitting there; there's no dialogue. Not that he was that strict or mean to us, but he was like a genius at work and we all

48

wanted to see, "Now, what does all this mean?" It meant a lot, because he might take a half an hour or forty minutes, not just with saxes, but tuning the whole band. He'd go to the trumpets; he'd go to the trombones; make sure the rhythm section had it. Then he'd come around and hit a few chords.

Lloyd took his time, tuned the band up, and made sure that the people were listening and that they would be team players, which is a whole other side to having a good band. A lot of times there's extra talent there, and in the case of a good soloist, it should be utilized. But the teamwork sets up something that's special, and he showed us that. You didn't come to rehearsal unless you were concerned about that, because a lot of times there were no solos for you. But guys would say, "Did you hear what happened when we finally all got on that note and it worked and the vibratos were alike?" So it was very special stuff that you don't hear very much today, but it can make a difference in the way the band sounds.

This approach to the band was something to hear – a band where intonation is a primary thing. To have a jazz band with intonation like that, it was scary. Those are the bands that we rave about. They have the feeling; they have the intonation, everything. A good Basie band, a good Ellington band had all that, of course. A lot of other bands that had the creativity didn't have the musicianship to pull it off, were a little sloppy. Lloyd's bands were never sloppy. We didn't do anything with the band except rehearse, but it was a pleasure to go and get that.

It was so good with Lloyd that we'd all begun having trouble – Mingus included – when we'd play other places, because we'd try to do the same thing.

"The band's out of tune," we'd say.

"What do you know?" They'd say. "You don't know anything."

"Well, Lloyd Reese said – "

"You tell Lloyd Reese . . .!"

He was a good influence on us because he was right most of the time. Once we came to him with a Jimmie Lunceford record, who we thought had the greatest band. Lloyd said, "I love the arrangement and everything, but it would have been nice if they had tuned up before they played." He was into reality and calling it like it is. When you do that, you can really get into the music. It was not how much you played, it was how you played it, and we became aware of that.

We used to spend a whole day on one chart, maybe eight bars here and then, "Let's do this." By the time we got through with that one chart, we hadn't had a chance to swing it and enjoy it. That would be it. It was almost like, "Gosh, if we could just play it through and enjoy it!" That's not the way he approached it. It was mainly a learning experience for us, to see what we could do.

When I get my bands together, I'm not the same way that he was, but I'm a real stickler for intonation, people playing together, watching the balance and the shading, and all those things that are a part of it. I hear too many musicians who are not aware of what makes one band better than the other. Of course, the arrangements are important, too, but it's how the players perform together and what they bring to it, which is even more important. I heard bands like Jimmie Lunceford's when he lost all his key players. The new guys came in and played the same music, and it was time for tears. It just wasn't going any place.

Lloyd was a marvelous teacher and everybody went to him – Eric Dolphy, Dexter Gordon, Bill Douglass, me, Mingus, Bob Farlice, the McNeely brothers, Bob Cooper, Lamar Wright, Eddie Davis, James Robertson, Jake Porter, Jack Trainer – I could go on and on. Even Ben Webster would come over and take lessons. There was a bunch of us who came from that school, but we never threw his name around that much. The ones who went to Lloyd Reese all did very well, because they could go anywhere. It wasn't just that they could play their instruments well; they had to be able to meet with people, and conduct themselves properly. They knew how to make time and they were concerned about the whole orchestra. It wasn't just, "Well, I played mine," but, "Guys, could we all get an A? Could we all tune up again? Could we all maybe play a little easier?" That was a Lloyd Reese-type student.

Once I had a date with Percy Faith. We were going to do "What Are You Doing for the Rest of Your Life?" The day before the date he called me.

"I want this husky sound that they're doing today, that the new guys are playing. Can you do that?"

"Well, I think so."

"I've got a tenor solo for you, but I need that husky sound."

I got to the date and he saved this number for last. It was Michel Legrand's tune, beautiful tune, great trombone solo in the beginning. He started me on the fourth-line D. All of a sudden it came to me and he stopped the band, all forty-five musicians, after I'd played about two bars. He said, disgusted, "I thought you knew this husky sound that they're playing. I called you on the phone and you said. . . ." He wanted to really punish me, now that I had let him down.

I said, "You did say husky sound, but why did you write it on the middle D? For me to play the husky sound, I would have to play that an octave lower. I was not going to change your music. If you'll allow me to play it an octave lower, I think you'll get the sound you wanted."

We went back, played it again, and the orchestra loved it, because now I was matching wits with this master. But I knew what I was talking about and I gave him a subtle lesson, because you can't push those guys too much. Don't try to make them look bad. But there you go: a Lloyd Reese-type student.

Twenty years old and on top of the world

When I was about twenty, I joined Cee Pee Johnson's band. Cee Pee had been playing in Lionel Hampton's band. When Hamp left to join Benny Goodman in New York, Cee Pee took over as leader. A few years later Marshal Royal and Jack McVea left Cee Pee to join Lionel Hampton's first band, and he needed alto and baritone players to take their places. Cee Pee wanted Jack Kelson and I, since we were the new guys who could play, but Jack's parents wouldn't let him work. Kirk Bradford came in and tricked me into playing baritone. I was supposed to play alto, but he said he couldn't reach the low notes on the bari because his hands were so small. Lloyd Reese and Jake Porter were also in that band playing trumpet.

We played in Hollywood at places like the Rhumboogie, which was at Highland and Melrose Avenues. Cee Pee was very cool and always messing with his hair. One night Cee Pee was getting ready, taking his time, when owner Mickey Cohen came in very angry because waiters were stealing whiskey. When he saw that the band wasn't playing yet, he pulled a gun: "I'll give you three minutes to get the band on the stand!" He gestured to hit Cee Pee, who didn't even blink. We finally got out there and things got more out of hand. Two or three of Mickey's guys were hitting the waiters in the head with chairs. Mickey just locked the door and told the band to play while all the fighting was going on.

When Cee Pee would go into a club, he'd get the owner to put in a radio hookup, because he had an audience and the club would be packed. He'd put on quite a show and always attracted the stars and the producers. They loved his showmanship. Sometimes he'd turn to us and say, "Gimme some fat men," meaning he wanted some rich chords. So we'd be holding long notes and he'd sing "Waiting For Ships," pulling on his hair and crying, spinning around. Everytime, I thought he was going to flip out and go crazy. He'd fall on his hands, flat on the floor. It would become dead quiet and nobody moved for about thirty seconds. Then the music would start and Cee Pee would come up crying. All the stars would be looking at this guy, while we're just sitting there being cool. He had great nerve and he was talented. Whatever he wanted to do, he did it, usually very dramatically and very high. He was smoking pot and everything. That was Cee Pee Johnson. The music was fine, but the characters there were something else.

We also played at Hazel's in San Pedro. One night Kirk Bradford was driving us there. He was talking a lot and it was raining. Suddenly the car began to slide; Kirk hit the brakes and we turned over. It was dark; the horn was blowing; and we were upside down. I thought, "This is what death feels like." I didn't feel any pain and it happened so fast. Kirk was pinned in the front seat and I had been thrown in the back. Some of the other guys came along and ran over to see what had happened. They took us to San Pedro hospital, but we actually played later that night, starting about an hour late.

Cee Pee's band was in about two to three movies a year, films like *Citizen Kane* (1941), *Kitty Foyle* (1940), *Tom, Dick and Harry* (1941) with Ginger Rogers, and *You'll Never Get Rich* (1941) with Fred Astaire and Rita Hayworth. Orson Welles knew about our band and it was his decision to use us in *Citizen Kane*. We played a little blues number at a big party near the end of the film. It's a quick scene and in a dark setting, so it's probably hard to pick anyone out. Welles did something different in that scene. You never recorded on the set then, but he insisted that we play and that it be recorded with the scene. A lot of the work we did on film was mainly sideline, where you pretend to be playing, but it's our music in that film. We also played at a lot of Hollywood parties. They all wanted Cee Pee.

I first saw Nat Cole at the Rhumboogie. He did most of the writing for the shows at the club. He was always so straight, all the music was in order. This was when he had the trio with Oscar Moore and Wesley Prince, but he wasn't singing yet. He had a knack for writing that fit the chorus girls just beautifully. He was working the Radio Room on Vine Street and he'd come in just to hear how the arrangements worked.

Later on I was in Nat's band when he had a show on local TV. Just before one broadcast Oscar Peterson and Jimmy Bunn were on the set playing "Lush Life," and they couldn't get out of it. Nat was walking around the set, talking to people, fixing his collar. Finally, they called him over. "Nat, do you know what happens here?" He just sat down, played the whole thing, and then walked away from them. One night on the show, Nelson Riddle, the music director, was looking at his watch and studying the music. "Nat, we're about eight bars too long here." The show would start soon and he was almost in a panic. Nat was the coolest of anybody. "Well, Nels, why don't we do this. When you get to the letter C, have the band stop. I'll make a modulation and you guys come in at letter F." We were all frightened to death and he did it like there was nothing to it. Nat never pushed his knowledge on you, but he had it.

I also played the Club Alabam and a few other spots on Central Avenue. We were coming from high school into this big world where we were making a little money, maybe about thirty or forty dollars a week with Cee Pee, when my dad was only making twenty-five dollars. After three weeks I was able to buy a brand new 1941 Pontiac. The car cost $1200, but payments were about fifty dollars a month. I could do it and Jackie Kelson couldn't believe it. At first I was living at home, but then I moved away. It was a very exciting period for a young man. I'm nineteen or twenty and the chorus girls started to notice me. Five or six of the most beautiful women in the world wanted to ride with me in my new car. And they were into all kinds of good stuff – drinking, smoking a little pot. I should have said "no," but they were so pretty. I knew I couldn't go the party route, though, because I wanted to be a good musician and take care of my health. Two or three of these girls would ask me over for a late night dinner, but I had to get up early and practice for my lessons with Lloyd. It was beautiful to have something to keep you strong, and study did that for me at the time. The only problem was that we didn't know how long we'd work with Cee Pee. It wasn't like having a real steady job.

I joined Les Hite's band for an eight- or nine-day northwest tour in 1941. This was probably between dates for Cee Pee. Aside from the nationally known bands, like Ellington and Basie, work wasn't continuous, and you'd fill in with other jobs. The lead alto was Floyd Turnham. I played second, and Gerald Wiggins was on piano. Gerald Wilson and Snooky Young were in the trumpet section, and Gil Fuller wrote the arrangements. That band was dynamite and much better than most people knew. Les was a gentleman, a good human being, not a fabulous soloist, but a good musician and he wanted quality. Les thought a lot about his musicians. He would ask me what reed number a musician in the band would use. Then you'd come to rehearsal and there would be a box of reeds on your seat. We toured the northwest, Washington and Oregon, and he had a lovely lady financing the band. Without her we wouldn't have made that tour.

It was a fabulous period for a twenty-year-old with a brand new car, in the best bands, playing for the stars, and being in *Citizen Kane*. I was on top of the world.

5
The war years

When the United States entered World War II in 1941, we began to worry. A lot of my friends were being drafted. Then I heard that a chief from the US Navy had come to the musicians' union on Central Avenue to recruit musicians for an all-black US Navy Reserve band to be stationed near San Francisco in Moraga at the St. Mary's Pre-Flight School. It was almost guaranteed that we'd be stationed in the San Francisco area, unless there was a critical situation.

Charles Mingus, Bill Douglass and I grabbed a Greyhound bus from Los Angeles a week later to go to San Francisco for a physical and a music test. When we got there, Mingus changed his mind and tried to get out, saying he had a bad heart and couldn't walk, doing everything to get them to throw him out, and they finally did. At that time a lot of people would take something to run up their blood pressure to throw the doctors off. If your heart was beating a mile a minute, all of a sudden you'd be 4-F. Mingus did some of that. He didn't do well on the music test either, because he wasn't a good reader at that time. Those tests were always hard, but I did pretty well playing clarinet. So I figured, "Well, I got it. Maybe I should hang with it." Bill was a good drummer, who could read very well. He passed also, but on the way back to Los Angeles changed his mind and decided not to join the navy. Later he was drafted into the army, served in the cavalry, and ended up going overseas.

The Topflighters

I was sent to Great Lakes in Illinois for basic training. There must have been hundreds of musicians from all over the country, including many from the west coast: Marshal and Ernie Royal, Jerome Richardson, Wilbur Baranco, Andy Anderson, Quedellis Martyn, and many others. There was another guy, Herman McCoy – I don't think his name was McCoy then – who was a great choral director, the finest, and did a lot of wonderful things in LA in the fifties.

Two nights after we arrived, they had a big jam session. It was like a hello to everybody who was there, and there must have been hundreds of musicians. I'll never forget it. Clark Terry kind of ran things. You had twenty saxophones, sixteen trumpets and about fifteen trombones, all in this big hall waiting to introduce themselves musically. Even though you had seen many people, you hadn't heard anybody play. We all went around and played a couple of choruses on whatever tune they were playing, which was great. If you played well, you were a hero. People would want to know you based on how you sounded.

Marshal Royal came up to me and said, "We're building a band for when we get to the West Coast and I want you to play baritone sax." I hadn't brought a baritone with me and I didn't want to play it. I played baritone in Los Angeles only for a period when I was with Cee Pee Johnson's band at the Rhumboogie. Marshal just didn't want me playing alto, because he played alto. Every now and then people do that. So I said, "No, I don't think I want to play baritone anymore." Then he tried to get the chief to more or less order me to do it, but I wouldn't budge. "I don't want to play baritone. It's too heavy to be marching with." I used every excuse I could. So they left me out. They got a good friend of mine, Curtis Lowe, who was a tenor player, to play baritone.

From Great Lakes we were sent to St. Mary's Pre-Flight School, which was twenty miles east of Oakland, California. We had a band room and everything, and were instructed to find our own apartments. Since I wouldn't play baritone, they built the big band without me. I should have been in it because of the caliber of my playing. I was as good as many of the guys in the band, and there were some very good ones in there: Marshal, Andy Anderson, Que, Ernie Royal, Jerome, Jackie Kelson, Earl Watkins. I just didn't want to be in Marshal's band, because, as much as I liked him, I knew how he could be and I was right on target. Marshal was a toughie, especially if he's in charge of the group. He had the all-stars in his band, but he was dominating it. The solos went to Marshal and his brother, Ernie. He even did that later in the Basie band. There are a lot of stories of Marshal giving guys a bad time, even when he shouldn't have been, only because he was the straw boss.

The players who weren't in Marshal's band had to do all the dirty work, like mopping and playing for the colors – basically, band music for the cadets to march by – while Marshal's band set up for rehearsals and worked on some of Basie's arrangements and music like that. They played the cadet dances on Sunday. If they played on Sunday afternoon, they would be off all day Monday until Tuesday. We could be off Sunday, but we had to be in on Monday. If it was clean-up time, "Okay, Buddy, you and your guys." I was the leader of the marching band, so we played for the cadets. Marshal's band would play a Thursday night sometimes in San Francisco at the canteen or one of those affairs. The next day our group would be the only ones at the base. Royal's band would sleep in late, come in on Friday and talk about, "Ah, we live the life of a king." They had the lush life and we knew we were getting the short end of the deal.

After a while our guys began to think, "What can we do?" And we had some terrible players. *Terrible.* There were forty-five people recruited and Marshal took all the cream. We had a couple of guys who could play a little bit, but most of them were into everything else. Nobody was really into music. We had an alto player, a nervous guy named Orlando Stallings, who I called "Burg." He could hardly play and he kept coming to me, saying, "Man, I've got to learn to play this alto." Our chief, Al Sondy, was really on him, because he didn't like anybody who couldn't play. "If you guys can't hit it and play those marches with the right spirit, I'll ship you out." He hated the way we sounded even as a marching band. "That's the worst band." And here I am with the worst band.

Stallings was as nervous as he could be. He came to me and said, "Willie" – he called me Willie – "I don't know what to do. I've got to learn to play this saxophone."

"Well, you've got to practice for one thing. I'll teach you."

57

That's when I really started my teaching career. I taught a little bit before going in, but I really taught there. All the guys began to talk and soon I was teaching trumpets and trombones – everything. I taught the whole band, because we realized that we were getting shafted. It was a great thing to see this happen. It really taught me a lot of ideas that I'm using today. You can make it with whatever your team is, if the people have the right attitude and work hard. Of course, there has to be some talent there somewhere.

After we did the colors at eight o'clock in the morning, we had three hours free; nothing until noontime. So I started Burg Stallings practicing during this time. We couldn't practice inside the barracks, because it was for the other guys – "Marshal Royal and His Bombardiers." We had to practice outside. I used to take Stallings about half a mile or so up in the hills, sit him under a tree with his music stand, and have him doing long tones to build up his embouchure. After a while he began to play in time and got much better. Stallings' tone was big and strong, and at first I didn't even realize it, since he was playing outside.

Next we had a trumpet player, James Ellison. I called him "Georgia Boy," because he was from Georgia. He was a nice guy, but a little dense in a way. He was very forgetful. I began to station him out there as well. He did his long tones, then lip slurs, thirds and fourths. Soon I had all these students standing on rocks and under trees doing long tones and exercises. The guys in Marshal's band saw us there and thought I was crazy. Well, you can imagine, it was a funny sight. "What are they doing?" Ten or fifteen of them out there, but they took it and everybody was practicing. Our first trombone player, George Lewis, learned to play very well in a short time. I called him "Fat Boy."

I nicknamed everybody and the names all fit. We had another trumpet player, Myers Franchot Alexander, and we called him "Bandmaster," because he was a little guy who always seemed to want to lead. He drank a lot, but was still the neatest one of all of us. He could be blind drunk over the weekend, and on Monday, with the bloodshot eyes and everything, his stripes were just perfect, shoes perfectly shined. What a combination! One guy, a bass player, we called "The Indian." If he'd drink a little bit, he'd want to tear the place up. "The Bear" was playing bass tuba. He was actually a barber named Ralph Thomas. One of the tenor players was a very wiry little guy with bow legs. We called him "The Spider." Another tenor player was "The Crow," a short, very dark guy, about five foot, fat, and with a very pointed chin. Henry Godfrey was one of the trumpet players and he was called "The Duck," because of the way he walked.

This was our band. Soon we started rehearsals, and after three months of this I still didn't realize how good they were getting. Then some of them asked, "Could we start a band?" So I got some stock arrangements, like "All or Nothing at All" – nothing hard. We started playing and it sounded very good. I couldn't believe it; we were seeing results. The first trumpet player by this time had such a sound, and my lead alto had such a sound it was scary. We started playing these stocks and it was really a pleasure standing there listening. We tuned up properly all the time and everybody was in sync with each other. If I'd say something, they wouldn't horse around at all. It was really great, because they all accepted it.

We built it up to where it was sounding very good, and then we started rehearsing every day. They wanted to, and if they wanted to, of course I wanted to. I wasn't playing that much, but I was conducting them. Every day at rehearsal we'd run over the music and try a new one, always slow stuff. We never played anything hard. I arranged things like "In a Persian Market," or an original. Everything we wrote was simple, but simplicity is still the key to most things. If it can be simple and swing and have good people playing it, you've got it. The other band still wasn't aware of what we were doing, because we'd rehearse further away so we couldn't hear them.

One day we were playing, sounding very good, and I was thrilled. We had about four or five numbers we could do now and they really sounded good. All of a sudden I looked up and there was the captain of the base, Captain King, with a bunch of gold braids he'd been showing around. He walked up and said "Wow! That is wonderful music you're playing there. I've never heard of this band. I'm aware of the Bombardiers, because they play for our dances, but I'm not aware that we have another band here." He actually liked what we were doing better than what they were doing! He just wasn't into their swing thing and this was just a dance band. "I love it. I'm going to have to speak to the chief, because I would like to have this band play some of the affairs." Nobody knew this would happen. I hadn't thought it could happen either.

When we got back to the barracks, there was the captain with the chief: "I just heard your other band. I'd like them to share duties with the Bombardiers." They split all the work with us. Those other guys were so angry; Marshal was angry. They didn't know we could pull that off. I wasn't a talker and I wasn't trying to outdo anybody. I never was. It just happened that we were doing our thing and the captain liked our sound. It was a pretty sound, not great, but not bad. Even our guys couldn't believe this band could play that well.

Now we had to get a name, so we called ourselves the Topflighters. We played many of the affairs, like cadet dances on Sunday. *We* had Monday off now and *they* had to mop the floor. So we reversed the tables on them and partly because those guys did that hard work.

It was a crazy period of seeing what teaching was; how these players came from nowhere in a few months just doing the necessary things. Most of them never got to be too fast, but the trombone player, George Lewis, got so good on first trombone that Marshal Royal took him into his band to play first trombone. He was a sharp guy and is a doctor somewhere now.

Marshal and I had different approaches to running a band. When we played jazz, my approach was to try and let everybody have a little piece of the pie and get exposure. Even when they couldn't solo, I'd write something for them to play on. Marshal's approach was more or less to dominate the band, which doesn't work as well for me, because after a while the players aren't giving you all of themselves. They're just sitting there, putting in the time, and all the guys in the Bombadiers could play. So Marshal kept them from expressing themselves. For example, he had two great tenor players in his band, Quedellis Martyn and Andy Anderson. They'd be going through a Basie arrangement with a tenor solo in the middle of the chart. Marshal would say, "Very good, very good. Let's play it again, but I'll take the tenor solo." You can open arrangements up; you can leave the tenor solo in and still repeat that chorus, but Marshal would take that solo away from the tenor player. In that way you hurt your people and then they'll only give you so much. Jerome Richardson and Jack Kelson didn't solo very much, and that's what I knew in the beginning. I liked Marshal, but that's the way he was.

Willie Humphrey, who was a great clarinetist, joined us later. He was about forty then. He was from New Orleans and played at Preservation Hall. He and a couple of other guys were brought into the concert band. They couldn't find a place for him in Marshal's band, so I took him into the Topflighters and let him play some solos. Willie Humphrey was a very humble guy and he just said, "Thanks for letting me play with your band." Marshal didn't pick up on how to utilize his talent, because Willie played Dixieland. We found places and music for him to play, and it was wonderful to hear him. So I utilized everything. It didn't bother me.

Although most of us hadn't planned on getting married at the time, that's what happened during the war years. We'd bring our girlfriends in, but there was no living together. After a year or so most of us got married. If you liked your girlfriend, you had to have something serious in mind. It wasn't just "Come stay with me for a weekend." They'd get back home and their mother and father would say, "We can't have this. You can't go."

Louise had also grown up in the Watts area of Los Angeles, but we didn't really meet until a few years later, just before the war, when I was starting to work as a musician and she was a dancer at the Club Alabam. One night we met at a party and started going out. The war separated us, but like most of the couples, we finally decided to get married and lived up in the San Francisco area until the end of the war.

Most of the musicians who wanted to play were able to work in a lot of clubs around the San Francisco Bay Area, even though we weren't supposed to. When you're in uniform, you're not supposed to be working outside. We got a job in Redwood City, about twenty-five miles south of San Francisco, playing jazz. So we would get in civilian clothes. It was such a good job, about two nights a week or so, and we were able to do that in 1944 and 1945. It wasn't the money so much, as the chance to play jazz and keep up on our instruments.

We heard a lot of music and musicians in Oakland. There was Sweet's Ballroom, where you would hear all the big bands. There was the Oakland Auditorium, where we used to hear Benny Carter's band or Jimmie Lunceford's band, Tiny Bradshaw, or Tommy Dorsey. All those bands would come through and we were always there.

Although we spent the duration in the San Francisco area, from 1942 until January 1946, we were able to get to LA periodically. I still had that 1941 Pontiac and we'd drive down maybe once or twice a year. The last time was to hear Bird and Diz.

A night at Billy Berg's, December 1945

Before we got out of the service, Ernie Royal and I drove to Los Angeles to see Dizzy Gillespie and Charlie Parker, when they opened at Billy Berg's in Hollywood. That band was Ray Brown and Milt Jackson and Al Haig and Stan Levey, and then, a little later, Lucky Thompson. We had been impressed by the records we'd heard and had to drive down. Opening night was really fabulous; the place was packed with people. It attracted most of the LA musicians and they all came to hear. This was for real. What you'd heard on the records that you didn't believe, you had to believe now, because you saw people standing there playing it.

Bop was kind of scary to hear, because they were playing so fast, a lot of notes. We didn't understand what they were really playing. When we'd put on the records, everyone would stand around wondering, "What are they doing?" It was just going so fast and so right, and the phrasing was right there. They were using flat nines and flat fives. You can go into different scales and pick them up much easier than to just figure out what they are. Just playing those scales with them, all of a sudden you're making the piano player get out of your way. And the piano comp was sparse; they weren't ringing through it, which made things work. A lot of piano players like to grab everything on the downbeat and hold through. Of course, if the group has something that the piano doesn't have, that's not going to work. But if the piano player plays you something short, you can get away with a lot of things, as long as there is no clash. They were doing that with a lot of creativity and a lot of musicality. The tempos were scary to even handle those things. They were using notes that we didn't even dare use before, because it would be considered wrong, and those stops and gos, so rhythmic, between Dizzy and Bird. "Can you believe what we just heard?" That was the way it was and they were doing it like there was nothing to it. Then Bird would solo and he was masterful; his time was flawless. You could see he was a strong force. That's the way he played.

It affected us and all you could do was to analyze the tunes and try to figure out, "Are they that tough to play? Can I go that fast? Can I keep up with this pace?" If you see something or hear something, it's a constant learning situation and a constant change, which I like. Some people like to get something and hang on to it, but I think life is full of change. In hearing them, no matter what you had learned, here was some other stuff that you could add. It was very enjoyable to me. Not that I wanted to play exactly like they did, but I wrote out a few of those tunes. It was a lesson that you need. Can you play those lines on your horn? If you can play those kinds of lines, it gives you a different set of chops, fingers, or coordination. And to play it from memory, too. To read it is one thing; to memorize it, I think that means you know the sound of the horn better, because you're going for the sound rather than "I know that is an A I'm playing." They were utilizing memory work and in the jazz field that's king. So of course we were impressed, because we saw them playing that amazing music with no music in front of them.

6
Post-war Central Avenue

By the beginning of 1946, I had been away in the navy for almost four years and I wanted to come back to Los Angeles to see if I could make a living as a musician. I had one child at the time, William Zan Collette, born in 1944, and my wife, Louise, who I married up north in 1943. We figured Los Angeles was our home and both our families were here. Her mother had a big house and we stayed there for a while, before we got an apartment. It worked out okay, but it never works too well with the in-laws. I was beginning to practice regularly and had started studying using the GI Bill. I could play clarinet and saxophone pretty well, but I figured that if I was going to make it in the music business, I had to be very good. My mother-in-law thought, "This guy's wasting time. Why doesn't he go out and get a job?" She also tried to influence my wife. They didn't understand. I couldn't convince them that I knew what I was doing and it was a period when I didn't have a lot of money.

The sounds of the Avenue

When I came back from the service, there was a big change in the Eastside area. The war years had brought a booming economy and also an awareness that people could do more than just what they were doing before. The black community began to expand and venture out.

The clubs along Central Avenue were flourishing. People were out living it up a little bit, dressing great. The Club Alabam had chorus girls and orchestras. About this time Johnny Otis opened there with his big band; it sounded a lot like Basie's band. Across the street Big

Jay had a group – he was Cecil McNeely then. Big Jay was a very hot jazz player, a very fine jazz player. He can still play jazz, but he knows where the money is and he's got a show business act going for him now still playing rhythm and blues. When Bird and Diz came to town in '46, Jay and Sonny Criss had a band and, man, they were doing all the stuff that Bird and Diz were doing. It was a hot group with Hampton Hawes on piano, Buddy Woodson on bass, and Leon Moore, the drummer. Later on, Jay got with Johnny Otis and they began to do rhythm and blues, and Jay moved away from bop. The Lorenzo Flennoy Trio was working in a small place. There were many clubs up and down the Avenue. The Jungle Room was across the street from the Lincoln Theatre at Twenty-third and Central. The Lincoln Theatre had big shows: the Will Mastin Trio with Sammy Davis, Jr., and Pigmeat Markham, the stand-up comedian. Lucky Thompson had his big band there later. And a few months later I was at the Downbeat with the Stars of Swing.

There wasn't much trouble between black and white. At the jam sessions there weren't a lot of white musicians, but there was Kendall Bright, who was a trumpet player. Art Pepper would come, although I didn't see Art very much. Kenny would walk in any place and be great. He just looked like: "Hey, it's cool." I think the only trouble was with the cops. The law enforcement people didn't like seeing too much mingling, especially with all the white women who would come down. The cops would give them a bad time. They'd say, "Stay out of here. If you're caught in here, we'll run you in for something." They tried to make it illegal just for being there, and it seemed after the war that it was happening even more.

One thing that didn't change was that there was still a lot of musical variety on the Avenue; more variety in the music than you hear today, because now it's marketing. They didn't market then. Central Avenue was a place where you could bring your own ideas to the stage, to the audience, whatever they sounded like. You were not being judged because you didn't sound like this or that musician. Now there's more of that. There's a certain way that you should play, or a certain horn or mouthpiece that you should have. Then you're "in." On Central, if somebody had a different approach, it was well accepted. Creativity was at its highest level. Your concern was: "Can I think of something different, a different way to approach this? Then when I go into the session on the weekend, I'll really wow them." There were not too many rules to be broken in music at that time. I think it was easier just to be you. We all respected each other and we didn't all want to play like each other. The charm of it was that you came in with your own sound.

At the time the tenor players, even the great tenor players, were all sounding so different. You heard Lester Young, that was one world; Coleman Hawkins was another; Ben Webster was somewhere in between. You knew exactly who was playing. There were many styles around at the time in Los Angeles: Dexter Gordon, Teddy Edwards, Wardell Gray, Gene Montgomery and Big Jay McNeely. Close your eyes and you could tell who was playing. For alto players, it was the same thing: Sweet Pea Robinson, Sonny Criss, Eric Dolphy and Frank Morgan. No way could you miss it; four bars or whatever and you could hear it. Bill Green and I were around; we were different. Jackie Kelson was different than me. We all hung together, but we never had the same sound. No one had the same tone or the same approach and it was very enjoyable to hear that; it was exciting. Just like when you pick up the phone and somebody says, "Hi," and right away you know, instantly, the first word, who it is, rather than saying, "Now, wait a minute."

Jam sessions were all over town. You'd go from one place to another. Sessions were going at Jack's Basket Room every night at Thirty-sixth and Central. We'd go there after-hours, when all the other clubs were closing down. That was when the Basket Room was really clicking. There was always gonna be a jam session until four or five in the morning and everybody would come with their own story. Wardell Gray and Dexter Gordon would meet up to jam almost every night, just like two fighters. Guess who won every night? Wardell Gray. Except after eight nights or so, Dexter would come in playing something very different. He was the most creative of the two, but also the most inconsistent. He couldn't do it every night.

We lived in the area and every night there was music to hear. We had a chance to develop our creativity. There was interplay. We were in a place where everyone was saying, "Create something. Give me something." That's why it was very enjoyable, because we knew the importance of having your own thing. I think at that time you were more respected for having your own ideas and maybe not for being great. The conviction of saying, "I'm going to play me" was something very special. And we didn't have the categories as much as they do now. T-Bone Walker and Pee Wee Crayton, all of them played at the Last Word and the Downbeat. It was all a pretty good mixture. You'd find a jazz tenor player sitting in with T-Bone.

It wasn't a matter of someone having to be really great to be in the swing of things, or that you had to be the best player before they would let you join a jam session. They'd just let you in to play on the third number or so, and I think that as a young player, it was a great thing to know that you would have a chance. That inspired a lot of the players.

There was something wonderful there.

The Stars of Swing

Shortly after I returned to Los Angeles in January 1946, got my feet on the ground and started studying a little bit, I got with Mingus and began putting a band together. Lucky Thompson was in town. He had done that gig at Billy Berg's with Bird and Dizzy, and he was rehearsing and working with Boyd Raeburn's band. We got John Anderson on trumpet. Trombonist Britt Woodman was here, as well as drummer Oscar Bradley and pianist Spaulding Givens, and they joined us. It was a perfect group of players, because everyone could really hold their own and most of us could write. Lucky wrote well, but he also brought arrangements from Jimmy Mundy, one of the top writers, who wrote for a lot of big bands. Lucky had Jimmy write things for seven pieces, four horns and three rhythm, and on that we built the band.

Spaulding Givens wrote beautiful things, very difficult to play because of the way the parts interchanged. We really had to have it well worked out. At first, as we played Spaulding's music, it didn't make sense to us. It was there; we just couldn't get into what he had, because the lines would break off and somebody else's line would pick up. The writing was very intricate and required a lot of teamwork. By the time we had played one of his pieces four or five times, it would come to us. Spaulding wrote probably the most unusual arrangements of all of us.

He was a very serious guy and looked like a professor. Little guy, probably weighed 145, 150 pounds, with a nice smile that would light up when the band played well. He wasn't a technical wizard at the piano doing lots of runs. He was mainly into chords and voicings, voice leading, but he would always keep it very interesting the way he would voice a piece. When he was comping, you never knew where he was going to be, very unpredictable, which was exciting. He would listen to what the soloist was saying and then give nudges – an extremely sensitive player.

Our drummer was Oscar Bradley, a fine drummer and another quiet guy. He'd rather be in the dim light than in the bright lights. He lived near Fourteenth and Central in an area that was not too cool and stayed in a little old apartment building, even when everyone else had gotten out and moved to another area. He dressed very sharp and played the drums very well, never dull and always tasty. He liked to stay in his groove, stay high, his own little world; he loved to play the brushes and had a great beat. With Mingus on bass, we had a very interesting rhythm section, very modern in a sense.

John Anderson, a handsome guy, who outdressed all of us with his pinstripe black suits, played trumpet. We found him working in downtown Los Angeles. John played very expressive with a little cry, nice like Clark Terry. He was always doing something with the notes, which made it interesting to listen to him. He wasn't always out-playing everybody, but any time he played it was a musical statement. With Lucky, Britt and myself, we had some horn section.

We started rehearsing at Mingus' house around Forty-eighth and McKinley every day for about three or four weeks. We'd have lunch together, come back and blow another two or three hours. This went on every day; nobody was going anywhere. If you had a lesson somewhere, you'd say, "I've got my lesson at three, but I'll be back."

We rehearsed and rehearsed, and we talked shading, and we soloed. We really worked on dynamics. We got so good, it was scary.

We wanted to play pretty stuff, a lot of ballads. I wrote a thing called "I'll Remember April." It was a bop line, but it was a smooth line for us. Our concept was musical with four-part voicing. Diz and Bird weren't doing that. In fact, the reason Lucky Thompson was hired to play with them at Billy Berg's earlier that year was because Billy Berg was unhappy with Diz and Bird's sound. He wanted it to be warmer and that's what he wanted Lucky to add. So our concept was to do the pretty things and Mingus was using the bow a lot on bass. We were definitely a departure from what was going on with Diz and Bird.

Then we invited over two guys from the Downbeat: Black Dot McGhee, the manager, and Harold Stanley, the owner. A few years earlier, Stanley had managed the Rhumboogie in Hollywood for Mickey Cohen. The Downbeat was the hot spot on the Avenue. Man, it was jumping in 1946. They listened and said, "What is this we're hearing?" We knew it was great, but we didn't know what the people were going to say. "You're hired! When do you want to open up? Next week?"

We decided to put a sign in front of the club and so we had to figure on a name. No one was the leader, so with a corporate idea in mind we settled on the Stars of Swing. "We're all stars and we swing." A couple of us went to the sign painter and said, "Here are the names of seven people. Make us a sign that says 'Stars of Swing' and just put these stars anywhere with a name in each one." That was a Monday night. Our opening was on Tuesday. We arrived that night, all happy, walked up and saw that the sign had been changed to "Lucky Thompson and the All Stars." Mingus wanted to kill him, of course. "What are you doing, man?"

Lucky said, "I'm the one with the biggest name, and I'm the best player."

We were just outdone. The people were waiting; we're in the back arguing. It took all the fight out of us. The band still played its can off. We were so good that we were probably up to 100 percent, if you can imagine that, and we dropped down to about 90 percent.

With most of the groups, you're only getting about sixty or so anyway.

Lucky still played his can off that night, but he wasn't a team player anymore and now he knew he'd blown it. But Lucky was like that; Lucky was for Lucky. He was very good on his instrument, but I knew that you cannot make it by yourself. We had a big meeting later that night outside the club and Mingus still wanted to fight him. Then we looked in the alley and found the original sign.

The next night we took down Lucky's sign and put back the Stars of Swing sign. When Lucky came to work that night he was less of a player. He wasn't going to play the real Lucky, and the third night he didn't show up at all. We called in Teddy Edwards at the last minute, who was a very good player, but he hadn't been with the group and this was a team effort. So we faded away, just that one gig for six weeks. We recorded Spaulding Givens' arrangement of "Laura," but never got anything out. We did it just for our own benefit.

Archie Moore, the light heavyweight boxing champion, told me that he had his ups and downs with Lucky Thompson. They would travel together in Europe. Archie would take Lucky with him, pay all his fees. He was the champ and he would be visiting these countries promoting his fights. Archie would be introduced as the champ. He'd take his bow and say, "And by the way, we have Lucky Thompson here, one of the greatest tenor players in the world." They did that all over Europe. When they finally got to one place, they walked into this club that was packed. Bud Shank and Bob Cooper were playing. They're from Los Angeles, of course, and they recognized Lucky before they recognized Archie. They said, "Well, we've got one of the great tenor players with us, Lucky Thompson." Lucky took his bow and forgot the champ, didn't even acknowledge him. This hurt Archie.

Before Archie fought Rocky Marciano for the heavyweight title of the world, Lucky told Archie, "You can beat this guy." They had an agreement that after the fight they'd meet at the club where Lucky was working with his band. They put up a sign: "The champ will be here after the fight." Archie did very well, knocked Marciano down –

nobody knocked that man down – but he didn't win. Archie left before the post-fight party to go see Lucky.

Everybody said, "Archie, come to the party."

"No, I promised Lucky."

He had to be at Lucky's gig; that was all he was thinking about.

When he got to the club, Lucky was just finishing playing and was very disgusted, because he heard the news. He took the tenor, threw it down on the stand, ran up to Archie and said, "Hey! Did you throw that fight, man?" Archie said tears ran down his eyes and he couldn't answer. Then Lucky told Arch, "The difference between you and me is that even on my bad days I'm still better than anybody else." Archie realized that this man was not in his corner and walked out. It was a big turning point.

Archie found out the hard way, like a lot of us did, that Lucky was for Lucky. His approach to life and people was: "I'm better than them, so I deserve the best." He was very good on his instrument, but I knew that you cannot make it by yourself. Finally, your phone isn't ringing; there are no jobs for you to play and you're out there alone. He wanted it all on his own terms and finally people said, "We don't need you." And when nobody needs you, baby, you got some trouble. That's sad. Maybe that's the lesson we all can learn: you can be the best, but you've got to have people to pull it off.

One year Lucky was on a Norman Granz-produced European tour of all-stars that included Louis Armstrong and many others. At one stop there were a lot of fans at the airport and Norman was trying to figure out the order people should leave the plane. He thought, Pops first (the musicians called Louis "Pops"), then the others. Lucky started arguing that he should go off first, that Pops had had it anyway. The musicians on the tour wanted to kill him.

Lucky would scare you to death with his technique, but he had no heart and feeling about people. More and more I look back and say there's no reason to remember him, other than that he got around on his horn.

Bird used to come to the Downbeat every night to hear the Stars of Swing when he was in town. We had a marvelous group, probably heads and shoulders above anything that had been on Central

Avenue, as far as an organized group with dynamics and the best musicianship goes. People were just spellbound because we had all the shading, the dynamics. I think that set the pace for a lot of things in the LA area. We brought the experience of guys like Mingus and me from the Watts area, who had been influenced by the Woodman brothers: an organization, not just a jam session. I mean shading, section work, looking nice on the stand, and being businesslike. Lucky had a lot of that also, but his ego hurt him. You've got to be a good team player before you can get to the top. Then maybe you'll be a good leader. Count Basie was not always a leader; he took over Bennie Moten's band, for example. Benny Carter was with McKinney's Cotton Pickers and Fletcher Henderson's band. They worked their way up and, finally, if it's your chance, fine.

We invited all the record company people to come and listen. Some came, but not one record appeared, not one inch was published about us. Now you can't prove we ever happened.

7
Branching out

Becoming schooled

After the war, I had the GI Bill and went back to school. There were many new musicians in town, like Bill Green and John Smith from Kansas City, and Stan Getz; and many had the GI Bill for studying. Schools were opening up and many of them music schools. The Central Avenue players, even before, were not into a lot of schooling. Some of us had Lloyd Reese and some who came from Jefferson High School had Sam Browne as a teacher, but many of the club players on the Avenue couldn't read very well. On many of the jobs you didn't have to read at that time, but you had to know the tunes from memory. The business hadn't changed as much into studio work, where everyone must read, and there wasn't work for minorities in a symphony orchestra. The main thing then was, if you had a little gig and it was paying the right money and the group was swinging, you were in.

With the GI Bill I got four years of study for free, as well as books, metronomes, reeds and all the supplies I needed. I used to go down and get ten, twelve books – a couple on clarinet, a couple on alto, a couple on flute – and the government paid for all of that. All I had to do was find the right teachers. You could go with private teachers, if you wanted, or you could get into the schools. I had three private teachers and I attended the American Operatic Laboratory, the California Academy of Music, and the LA Conservatory of Music and Art near MacArthur Park, right at Seventh Street near Alvarado, where I met Bill Green.

Bill always had a horn in his hands, even then. One day, somebody from the school told me, "There's a guy over in the park playing clarinet. He sounds real good." Anyone playing in the park you always think of as being a street person or something like that, because you're always thinking, "He can't be well." I said, "Well, I'd better go see him," because I didn't want to miss anything. There was this guy, dressed sharp. He was always immaculate: buttoned coat, warm day or not. He acknowledged me, but kept playing. Then he stopped for a moment and we introduced ourselves.

"You sound good on the clarinet."

He said, "Thanks," and went back to working on his music. Then he asked me, "Do you know that tune?"

"Yes. Why?"

"Because Rudy Rutherford played it with Count Basie." And he went back into it. He wasn't rude or anything. He was just so involved and was trying to share where he was.

We got to be great friends, because he was a great player and we both had a lot of ideas that were quite a bit alike. I remember Bill was with two other friends: John Smith, a saxophone player, and Nat Rattler, a trumpet player. They were all from Kansas City and had the GI Bill to study in Los Angeles. They were all very serious musicians, lived together, and practiced all the time.

We started going to lunch to break up the day and talk a little, but they would never eat anything. When I asked them about it, Bill would say, "We're okay," and then not eat. Something wasn't right with this. Finally, I pinned Bill down. He said, "Well, our checks haven't come yet, and we didn't want to bother anybody." Those government checks would come late, and they said they would fix hash and rice and things like that. They weren't making it and still they looked so neat and clean, and they were just so proud. So I twisted their arms.

"Look, I can help you guys, because your check's going to be here within a week or two and then you guys can buy my lunch."

We got to be real close then. That was the start of a great relationship between us, especially between Bill and I, and we worked in a lot of bands together. We were the alto players in Benny Carter's band in the last part of the 1940s, maybe 1947, 1948.

So at the school I was meeting new players, a group of people who

74

were different from many of the Central Avenue club players. A lot of them were thinking school and studying instruments. That was the period, too, I took up flute. Bill, who was also at the Conservatory, took up flute at about the same time and with the same teacher, Miss Cipriano. Bill's saxophone teacher was Ben Kanter and I worked with Socorso Pirrola on clarinet. For saxophone I had a private teacher, Merle Johnston from New York.

After a while I left the Conservatory. One reason was because I'd be there all day. I was spending too much time in class and didn't have enough time to practice. I'd rather go to individual teachers and have the practice time. Then I'd work on Friday or Saturday night. So I backed away from the Conservatory.

I continued to study saxophone with Merle Johnston at his studio at 4992 Melrose near Western Avenue. He was the first big New York teacher who came out here. He taught some of the guys who are teaching now, like Joe Allard and Romeo Pinquay, the guys who used to do all the studio work. If you wanted to play saxophone, you would go to Merle. He was the king in New York, because he had all the saxophone players.

Merle's studio was the junkiest shop you've ever seen: about eight by twelve feet and full of huge speakers and piles of books, record players, horns, and trashy. When you went in there and he'd close the door, you felt like you were in a death chamber. At one time he had a microphone out front of the building, and when you got off the bus, he'd be able to hear you talking. If you said, "That Merle is full of shit," he'd say, "I heard you talking about me when you were at the bus stop." That was wild. Who knows why he did it; he was kind of nutty.

At the beginning he would have you blow, and he would finger while standing behind you to make sure that you were relaxed. When someone would come in real tense, he'd use that technique. He'd start fingering your saxophone and you'd be going all over the horn from top to bottom. Because if you got the right air stream going, the notes would be just popping out. Then he'd say, "Now, you see what's happening? You're playing all those notes you were having trouble with."

He was a brilliant guy, but he had you blowing six to eight hours a day, full volume, with the metronome. If you didn't do it, you couldn't study with him and he could tell when you weren't practicing. Merle would put records on and turn the speakers up. "Okay, let's hear you play out," and then he'd turn it up louder. "I can't hear you blowing. Blow!" He'd get you to the point where he knew you could be heard over a band, if the band was trying to crowd you. He might also say, "The mouthpiece is not kicking out. Give me that mouthpiece." He would open the tip of the mouthpiece and then he'd put that volume up on you. Every night you'd be blowing your little butt off. Then you had to figure out how to blow like that and still play something interesting.

Merle was right in that way, because the giants played pretty full. They didn't suck on their horns, whether it was Hawkins or Dexter or Bird. Once Bird played in my kitchen and I knew we were going to be evicted, because he played so strong, consistently strong. I'm not saying it was loud, because it was still so musical, an incredible kind of energy going into his horn, marvelous when you hear it.

If nothing more, with Merle you got a hell of a sound and you got your fingers going. In fact, it was almost like a production line: "Give me a year and you'll be out there doing it." But you paid dues, because to him that was the only thing you should have been doing.

You'd say, "Yeah, but my wife ..."

"Well, look now, are you going to be a musician or not?"

You'd get into trouble, if you didn't agree with him. He'd either want to throw you out, or he was through with you. But he was right most of the time. He did wonders for everyone that studied with him: me, Teddy Edwards, Eric Dolphy, Frank Morgan, Jewell Grant, René Bloch, and the Wilder brothers.

I stayed with Merle about three years, but I was in and out of there during that time. He would say, "You're doing fine. Then you leave and go out of town or something like that." Actually that helped me, to go out of town, because I'd learn other things, but it also would get me away from practicing like he wanted me to practice. Merle was trying to set everybody up like he heard it. That was the kind of guy he was.

I also had a private flute teacher, who was Marty Ruderman. It wasn't until about 1948, '49, '50 that the flute began to generate some interest. Even with the Stars of Swing at the Downbeat in 1946, I might play it on only one number and people would ask, "What was that you played?" It was never an instrument that had a foreground role, playing the lead by itself and soloing. So it was very rare before the late 1940s.

I played flute because I liked the sound of it. In the early part of 1946, I was sitting in my car one night and I heard a record by Alec Wilder, who was a great writer and composed modern woodwind pieces. The one that I happened to hear that night was featuring Julius Baker, a fine flutist from New York, and it had sixteenth-note phrases with wide intervals. I said, "Wow! This is the first time I've heard a flute with that kind of exposure." I could hear some possibilities with this instrument. There were things that hadn't been done that I wanted to try. That was why I started playing flute. About this time Lee Young made a record called *Route de Flute*, and Harry Klee, first flutist at Columbia studios, played a jazz solo on flute. That also inspired me.

I thought about it for a month and as life will have it sometimes, a guy who I knew, Clifford Burton, who used to play with Miss Alma Hightower's band, walked up to me and said, "Would you like to buy a flute? Mine is in the pawnshop, and I don't think I'm going to be able to get it out." It only cost me about forty dollars. We went to the pawnshop that day, shelled out the money, and I was with it the next day, or trying to be.

Miss Cipriano, the flute teacher, didn't like the flute. After a few months of lessons she said that I had to get a good instrument. I don't know whether she knew I played saxophone and clarinet, but she saw I was learning fast. She was aware of one for sale downtown and we went down together to check it out. She said that if I didn't buy it, she would. I still have it.

Later on I studied privately with Marty Ruderman until he moved to Palm Springs. Then I went to the American Operatic Laboratory to continue flute studies. They recommended I study with Henry Woempner, an outside teacher. He also worked at MGM, one of the top players. I didn't know him, but I went and studied with him. He was a great teacher and he really changed my entire thinking about flute playing.

With Cipriano and then Ruderman you'd develop a nice sound and you'd be good enough to go just about anywhere. Woempner was completely different. He didn't like anyone and he didn't like the way I played: intonation was not good; time was off. He chased everybody away except me, and he was ready to do that, but I was determined to find out if he really had something or was just nuts. He was very punctual. If I was two minutes late because of traffic, he'd say, "There are no excuses. You be here at two o'clock." Then I'd start playing and he'd stop me after two bars: "No, that high C was sharp." This guy had me walking on thin ice, but he knew what he was doing. He had me listening. Before Woempner, I thought I and everyone else was sounding okay. He changed that. Damn, nobody's ever challenged me like that. I started working. He'd say, "I want you to memorize this whole page for next week." Tough, very tough, and never a smile.

Throughout these sessions he hadn't played a note, and I still didn't know how good the top flutist at MGM was. Then one day he was very emotional for the first time, tears in his eyes. He looked at me and said, "My father told me I could never master this instrument. I wish he could hear me now." Then he picked up his flute and started trilling. It was like bells. I'd never heard anything quite like that. Of course, he had incredible technique, but his sound was something else. I'd never heard a human being do what he did.

While I was playing one day, he suddenly said, "Stop!" He wasn't mad. I asked what was the matter and he said, "You don't have to ever play any better than that. You'll impress most people out there, but it'll take you a little longer to get to me." I think he was doing what his father had done to him, but then he showed me some amazing things and said, "You can do all those."

One of those times he did play for me, he just ran through it. I was thinking that son of a gun is good. He looked at me and said, "You know, I didn't really play all of that right. I might have missed a note or two, but you didn't know it, did you?" I told him he was right. He said that you had to have such control that even if there is a note or two that didn't come out, no one would notice. And part of that control was standing up there like you're the king, because people will believe what they see. Most teachers never explained that part.

Henry got me in the Flute Club, which was a first because there were no minorities in that organization. It was powerful and had all the top flute players, about thirty of them, as members. I had a chance to be around all these giants of the instrument, including Hockenburg and Archie Wade, for a couple of years. At one gathering a member had written some amazing piece for thirty flutes and turned all the parts face down on a table. Each of us picked one and I chose the second part. This experience took me into another world and I learned what the flute was about. I also saw that most of these top players were afraid of Woempner, because he was a stickler with everyone and he was right most of the time.

Later on, at the beginning of one of our lessons, he told me that my GI Bill support had run out. Then he said, "Why don't we just keep going until one of us gets tired." After a few more lessons, he told me that he was going to move somewhere up north, giving up the studio scene. They had fired him at MGM. From what I heard, the problem was his personality, having to be right all the time and speaking up whenever the band was out of tune. If you're not the leader, it's very difficult to do that; people will put you down. So he left town and bought a hotel. A couple of months later they found him dead along a nearby lake. No one knows what happened. I hope he didn't do himself in. He was really an unhappy guy, but I think he had achieved mastery of his instrument and proven to his dad's memory that he could do it. If anyone came close to it, Henry Woempner did. But he lost his job, didn't have any students, didn't have anything, really. Maybe a broken heart killed him. He used to play that thing, man, and nowhere to take it, a bit like Lucky Thompson.

After the Operatic Laboratory I went to the California Academy of Music, which was in North Hollywood. I went there because I wanted to study writing, and there was a guy named Franklyn Marks, who had studied with Joseph Schillinger, a teacher who devised a system of teaching music through numbers. Schillinger was a musician, but was a mathematician by trade, who taught in the community colleges. He couldn't really write any jazz. They said he used to come around to the jazz clubs, where the musicians were jamming. He'd have this scratch pad and he'd be writing these numbers down. During an intermission he'd go meet the musicians.

"I'm Joseph Schillinger and I just wrote down what you guys were playing."

"What do you mean? With these numbers? You must be crazy!"

"No. This is the pitch and this is your rhythm."

He was writing out the rhythms and the tone pitches, too, using graphs, a complete system. His books came out and got a lot of publicity: *The Schillinger System of Musical Composition,* with graphs. For instance, there was a graph of the New York skyline and that would be a melody, or the skyline of Los Angeles could be another one, depending on what each pitch level meant and what note it would come out to be. I was very curious. I always tried to be a forward-thinking person. If something's new, I want to hear about it.

It was wild; just the rhythmic section will change your whole scope of playing. It was a different way of thinking; it put you on another level. And the rhythm stuff is probably even more important than the melody, although we remember the melody. The rhythm is like the foundation of your house. His system makes you explore lots of possibilities. Maybe out of one idea of a bar, or two or three number combinations, I might get thirty different bars or so. I may only like about ten of them for what I'm using there. Yet, I'm still ahead of the game, because the average person will only think up two or three.

Somebody mentioned to me that Franklyn Marks would be teaching at the California Academy of Music and I went to meet him, which was a real joy. I knew he had done a lot of writing for Stan Kenton, a lot of writing for strings. I loved him and he had me write some good things. There was another private teacher I went to briefly in the early fifties, Wesley La Violette, who was also teaching Shorty Rogers, Jimmy Giuffre, and Marty Paich. La Violette was a European writer and composer who was interested in teaching these jazz guys musical form. He had a way of structuring what they were writing in the European style. It was very predictable. Some people liked that and it was very commercial. A lot of the so-called West Coast Cool style reflected this approach.

However, I'm always looking for rhythmic things, too. The rhythmic structure is the foundation of almost everything. You can put almost anything on top of a good rhythm. If you have great chords with the same rhythm you're used to, it's not bad, but it's not going to make you want to make a phone call.

So this was a period of learning, experimenting, meeting a lot of people. It was also the period of the Crystal Tea Room.

Teaching and jamming with a new generation

Bill Green and I used to rehearse together all the time. We'd meet on a Thursday morning or afternoon at his apartment or mine. Bill liked to cook and would make pancakes or something. After eating we'd go for a few hours, have lunch, and go for a few hours more, alternating between clarinet, flute and saxophone duets. We were studying all three of them with different teachers, but we were pooling our ideas; we'd discuss the different methods.

We also wanted to do something more than practice together. So Bill and I started these regular jams in 1948 at the Crystal Tea Room, Forty-eighth Street and Avalon Boulevard, that lasted for about three months. To organize and oversee the sessions, we formed the Progressive Musicians Organization, which included, in addition to Bill and myself, David Bryant, Jewell Grant, Lawrence Moulder, Bobby McNeely, and Clarence "Tex" Thomas. We wanted to work with and help the younger players, and we figured we could do that better with a more regular, non-profit organization. So we rented the Tea Room for under fifty dollars on Sundays. The idea was to have jam sessions once a week so musicians could hear each other and exchange ideas. The word got out. Eric Dolphy, Big Jay McNeely, and Sonny Criss would come by. Soon we discovered many of the new players that we didn't know: Walter Benton, Ernest Crawford,

Kenneth Metlock, Sweet Pea Robinson, and Frank Morgan. All these young players came over.

I also met some of the new guys when I started teaching music at Jordan High School in Watts. I'd go down there three nights a week to teach a jazz course, a big band class really. And some of the guys would follow me down to take the class, like Horace Tapscott, who would be there with his trombone every night.

Frank Morgan was just fourteen years old in 1948 when he first came out here, and was playing very well. His dad, Stanley Morgan, played guitar with the Ink Spots. He also owned a club called the Casablanca. Stanley knew how to make money. When he heard about the Tea Room, he brought Frank over and he broke it up. He was a young, green kid, but he could really play at fourteen. He came every week and was a beautiful young man. I think some of the problems Frank had later – drugs and jail – came from being so good at that early age. And his dad was raising the kid by himself, and he was very busy. He did well with Frank, but it's just that at fourteen, fifteen, Frank was really on his own and out playing jam sessions with older guys, like Dexter Gordon and Wardell Gray. Soon he began to meet with people and go to parties. How will you hold up through that? You're meeting ladies early, who are sort of helping you to hang.

"Can we do this?"

"Can we go here and have this?"

He went along with a lot of that and there was dope. Frank studied with me and was with me a lot, but at the same time he was hanging with a different crowd of people.

After I studied the Schillinger system, I was teaching two or three guys: Frank, Jewell Grant. I didn't get Eric Dolphy into the Schillinger because he had studied with me before that period. Merle was the one who pushed me into it. When Frank went to Merle, which was later than Eric, Merle kept stressing that he should do the Schillinger system.

I didn't spend much time with Frank after that, but around the mid-1980s he came over and said he wanted to study flute. He was serious about it, but couldn't quite get into it. He must have been about fifty-three, fifty-four. It doesn't mean it's too late to start, but like anything it is more difficult. To get the sound and the finesse on the flute is difficult at any point.

Frank's experience with Merle helped him a lot. Merle used to set a fire under him, if you can call it that. With the problems he had with dope and everything, he'd miss lessons and he'd be late. You can imagine the reaction he got. Merle used to curse him out. "What are you doing?" he'd scream at him. A lot of that was good for him in a way, because even now he's playing well and trying to take care of business.

I also had some contact with Sonny Criss. When I was first coming home from the service during the war, Sonny and Big Jay would catch me. My mom would tell them when I was coming into town. They also lived in Watts. I'd get together with Sonny, talk to him and more or less point him in a direction. Big Jay didn't study with me until later. Sonny was a good player when I first met him, there's no doubt about it. He was a pretty good reader and was confident about what he could do. He was a little hard to get to; he just knew where he was going, especially during the early bop period, when he had gotten into that style very quickly. He'd been listening to the records and was playing Bird's fanciest style. Sonny was almost as good, just a little different. He was young, but he ate the style up.

However, being that good didn't solve all of his problems. He didn't do any studio work, just an occasional jazz gig or a concert. By the time he was forty-five, fifty years old, he still wasn't making any money and became very bitter. Sonny would get a call to work for fifty dollars and he wouldn't do that; he wanted one hundred dollars and he couldn't always get it. So it was a sad thing for him.

It was hard to send Sonny out on jobs. He didn't play like Eric or Charles Lloyd. Lloyd didn't study with me, but we were good friends. They doubled on flute and other instruments, and it was easier to help them. Usually a studio contractor will say, "Well, we've got clarinet or flute" or something, and you have to think of somebody who has been more of a serious student preparing to do jobs other than their own albums. Sonny's idea was to do Sonny Criss and solo. I don't think he even cared about being an alto player in a big band.

He did all right, but I think he sort of felt trapped after a while. You get that good, and then you have a family, a son, rent money that's due, and you've only got one gig on a Saturday night for fifty dollars. After a while you say, "What's going on?"

So my advice to most of the students who were close to me was to be versatile, have the doubles. A lot of times you can put them into a band. They won't be soloing and it may not be exactly what they want, but they are working and playing music. Some students of mine I directed to do some copying, do a little teaching, and most of my guys are still out there, doing something musically.

First recordings

By the late 1940s I was beginning to write more. I was also beginning to get in the studios on recording dates with people like Ernie Andrews, Gerald Wilson, and Benny Carter. I recorded with Maxwell Davis, who was a tenor player and had his own groups. He was a guy I had worked with when I was a young man, fifteen or sixteen. Maxwell used to have the band down at the Follies on Main Street. He was a good writer and became musical director for the Bihari brothers on their various record labels out in Culver City. There was also Ernie Freeman, who was a good violinist and pianist, as well as a good arranger. He had just arrived in town from Cleveland, worked with my group a lot, and became a friend. Later on, we'd make records together and start our own music publishing company.

Charles Mingus was still in town and doing a lot of his own music. We were writing a lot and experimenting with tunes. His "Baron Mingus Octet" sessions in 1946 for the 4 Star Record Company brought us together in the studio along with Karl George, John Anderson, Britt and Brother Woodman, Eugene Porter, Lady Will Carr, and Oscar Bradley. The recordings were produced by War Perkins, a local disc jockey who taught Joe Adams how to dj. He even gave Mingus his name.

"Well, we've got a Duke and a Count. Let's make you a Baron."

There was a local trombonist and later business agent in the musicians' union, named Baron Morehead, and that's where Perkins got the idea.

These recordings were done about the time of the Stars of Swing performances at the Downbeat, and with Mingus, John Anderson, Britt, Oscar Bradley, and myself, the core of this recording band was the Stars of Swing. The sound of the Stars was smaller than this group – we only had four horns at the Downbeat – but basically it was close. Mingus always liked that bigger sound if he could get it, and with this recording band he could get more harmony notes, with the baritone sax providing more of a bottom and the extra trumpet. So the Baron Mingus Octet recordings were a fuller sound, but the direction and style was very much the same as the Stars of Swing. "Honey Take a Chance with Me" was a Mingus tune we recorded. We also did one of mine called "Bedspread," which I had written for the Stars of Swing, and which we had performed at the Downbeat.

We did about half a dozen cuts that day or two with the Octet, and today they still sound very modern. At the time we recorded they never got much circulation or attention outside of southern California, and many of the older guys thought that the way Mingus wrote, in the notes and chords he used, was crazy. Bebop had just come in, but Mingus was creating something different from that. He was seriously into composing – the charts for this session were written out, except for the solos – and trying for new sounds. His music was experimental and very difficult for us to play. But he'd just say, "You can make it. You can make it," while writing high G, high A.

In 1948 and 1949 we recorded for Dolphin's of Hollywood. John Dolphin's record store and radio station at Vernon and Central Avenue was one of the few outlets for black musicians at the time. He recorded and did business with everybody musically, but he was a hard-pay guy. He was a great talker and would find excuses not to pay anyone. Mingus and I would try to get our money, and he'd say, "I gave you a chance to record, didn't I? You should be happy." Once he sent me to get my master from a guy out in who-knows-where. This guy said, "I can't give you the master, because he owes me too much money already." Later on, one of the guys he was doing business with killed him.

I recorded a two-sided 78 for the Dolphins of Hollywood label: "It's April," and "Collette." I used Jimmy Bunn on piano, Harper Cosby on bass, and Chuck Thompson on drums. I have the tape and it's still very good; it holds up well. I like the melodies. "It's April" was later recorded on Prestige by Wardell Gray and Art Farmer, and they called it "April Skies." That was the first record that I had done under my own name, but there was no money. However, I was still in my twenties and a first album was pretty exciting. It was played on the radio and that meant I'd arrived. No money in the pocket from it, but people began to hear about me.

That was my first experience of taking control. I had written the tunes; I'd picked the musicians and ran the session. That's a growing-up part of business that we all need. It doesn't mean the sooner the better, but at a point when you can play and conduct yourself pretty well, then it's studio experience.

In the late forties and early fifties there were still a lot of jam sessions in town. Bird, Miles Davis, and Lucky Thompson were here. Mingus, Miles, Lucky, and a bunch of us used to rehearse at Britt Woodman's house. We liked to get together and try different things. There was a lot of this going on.

This was a period when there was a change in music attitudes. People were experimenting and holding jam sessions and rehearsals everywhere; music was happening morning, noon, and night. Jimmy Tolbert would rent Normandie Hall at Normandie Avenue and Jefferson Boulevard, and hold a jam session with Eric Dolphy and Ornette Coleman. Lots of people would come out to hear live jazz, even though that wasn't our main purpose. It was like what we had done with the Crystal Tea Room. We knew we could attract people, but the goal wasn't to make a lot money, so much as to exchange ideas with musicians.

Matilda Collette.

Three years old in Wasco,
California, 1924

The Al Adams Band at the Elks Hall on Central Avenue, circa 1939.

Paul Robeson with the Cee Pee Johnson band at the Rhumboogie Club, Hollywood, 1941.

Cee Pee Johnson band on the movie set for *Tom, Dick and Harry* with Ginger Rogers, 1941

The Topflighters band from the St. Mary's Pre-Flight School in Moraga, California, performing at the Canteen in San Francisco, 1943.

Performing at the Jungle Room on Central Avenue, 1946.

Josephine Baker appearing at Humanist Hall, 1950, in support of the amalgamation of Locals 47 and 767 of the American Federation of Musicians.

With Groucho, 1952.

The Chico Hamilton
Quintet at Strollers, Long
Beach, California, 1956.
Photo: Howard Morehead.

The Buddy Collette Quartet, Los Angeles, 1956.

Corky Hale and Billie Holiday fall by Jazz City in Hollywood to catch the Buddy Collette Quintet, 1958.

Recording in Milan, Italy, 1961, with clarinetist Johnny Basso.

Leading Ella Fitzgerald's band at Basin Street East, New York, 1963.

Charles Mingus, *c.* 1970.

Appearing on Gerald Wilson's
KBCA radio program, circa 1973.

Celebrating "Buddy Collette
Day" at the Biltmore Hotel in
Los Angeles, January 23, 1990.
Photo: Leigh Charlton.

8
Eric Dolphy

Not a one-three-five kind of person

I didn't know Eric Dolphy until I returned to Los Angeles in 1946. He was nineteen, and I was twenty-four or twenty-five. He said he knew of me through Lloyd Reese. Eric was working at Lloyd's house, doing the clean-up and running errands for his lessons. He was also learning his craft, and Lloyd had him on piano, clarinet, saxophone, and listening to everyone. Eric used to come around the Last Word, the Downbeat, clubs where we'd be playing. He was always at the Downbeat to hear the Stars of Swing.

Eric was a young man with energy, a lot of ideas, and very creative. Music was very important to him his whole life, of course. I think that is what adds to fine musicianship and talent. A person's talent is a gift, but he spent time listening; he had a high level of appreciation. Most people would say, "Well, I like this one better than that." Eric liked everyone and that's a rare talent in itself, when you're appreciating a lot, because then you're picking up things. You're not filtering; you're not editing. Eric liked it all and he used what he wanted out of it.

He loved the outside notes, being different, altering chords. I think the time he spent on the piano helped him. That's always a great approach. I'd give him a couple of melodies and he would alter everything. He loved it, using different notes, even with a lot of his flute stuff. He used to get some interesting density in a few things that would be far out. That's the kind of thing he liked. He wasn't just a one-three-five kind of person. He loved all those strange notes to the point of being out there even when the tune didn't call for it. When he put that horn in his mouth, he was having fun. He'd load the guns on you and there he'd go. And that was Eric.

At first, Eric studied with me for about six months and then off-and-on over a ten-year period. He used to practice with me all the time and he was a joy to teach. You didn't have to teach him that much; he just loved it. Whatever you gave him, he'd approach it like you had given him a toy or a bowl of ice cream. It was fun and the fun was always there; he would smile when he played or practiced, just enjoying it. There's not too many that you meet that have the magic within their makeup. Yeah, he had the right attitude, had a great family; Mr. and Mrs. Dolphy believed in and supported Eric. He had good manners and upbringing, all good qualities. He was just a joy and I loved him.

Eventually I got busy with a lot of work and I couldn't spend the time with him. So I sent Eric and Frank Morgan, who was also studying with me, to Merle Johnston. With Eric and Frank all I had to do was kind of shape them, give them a few ideas. I finally thought, "Why not just send them both to Merle?" I knew he would help them. They both needed that little kick in the butt that you get from a teacher like Merle. I told Eric to study with him, but not for more than a year. After a year with Merle you'd start losing your identity. He'd have you blowing and in those books, and you'd get faster and to the point where you could read everything. But Merle would go on like this was the only thing that mattered. He wasn't a jazz player at all and he had a way of not letting you go, which meant he'd always have more books for you.

Merle was also living in the past at that point. He could teach you sound and help you develop great fingers, but he wasn't in touch with what was happening out in the field. Merle was teaching the same way he taught players during the forties, and it was the fifties. Not that it was so far off, but he thought he could control that part of the business by sending the good players out there to set the pace. It doesn't work that way. The pace is already going and you have to blend with it, if you want to make the money.

Eric had a lot of rough edges, but he had the ideas. The tone and intonation were not too good. I told him, "You don't need but a year. He'll straighten your tone out, teach you how to blow." Eric took that as golden. One year later Eric waved good-bye and it was just right.

Eric was playing alto, clarinet, and piano. Lloyd Reese had everybody play clarinet. Eric hadn't gotten into the bass clarinet yet. Merle helped him with the clarinet, fixed his mouthpiece so he could play it strongly. Merle would take that mouthpiece and open it up a little bit so he would get more of a sound. He was playing it like a saxophone almost. He could belt it, whereas usually with the clarinet you can't always do that. Merle also sent him to Socorso Pirrola for clarinet. Those guys all knew each other. If you studied sax with Merle, he would suggest Mr. Pirrola for clarinet and vice versa. I'm not sure when Eric started on bass clarinet, but Merle wanted you to play everything and he probably pushed it.

I also sent him to Russ Cheever and Dom Fera, both fine clarinet players. Russ was a principal saxophone/clarinet player at Twentieth Century Fox, and Dominic Fera was a principal clarinet freelancer, who always played in the top bands. I sent him to everybody that I thought was a good teacher, because Eric had energy: "What else can I learn? What else can I do?" I would say, "Well, go to this guy for a while and he'll give you some cues." I sent him to Elise Moennig, who started him out on flute and became his teacher. I didn't start him on flute, although we did a lot of stuff together. I figured he needed to have the basics. So Elise did a lot for him, gave him the good literature. Eric had what a lot of jazz players don't – a background in classical music. It was not always apparent, but he loved to practice it. He'd spend more time practicing classical than jazz, so he had the fingers and had the difficult things always behind him. He could just dance off those kinds of things.

I don't deserve the credit for Eric, because he was playing notes a mile a minute. Part of it was Lloyd Reese in the early days and later on with Merle, getting the sound and everything. When we did the concert with Mingus at Town Hall in 1962, Eric was probably the fastest and the best reader. And he was one of the most comfortable, because he had worked a lot with Mingus' music, which gave him a little advantage, but he also had this background.

Trying to make it in LA

After a while people began to notice Eric. He didn't have many gigs, but, "Hey, the guy's really playing." It was like having a diamond that you're always just sending in for polishing. It's great, except no one can see it. When we did a session for a lady named Fran Jeffries, I had him on baritone sax – around then he began to play baritone pretty well, too – and I had Calvin Jackson on the piano, a band of about eight pieces. Fran Jeffries was a great singer at the time and one of the most beautiful women. A lady who was managing her, Ann Dee, used to have a club called the Blackhawk in San Francisco. Ann called me around 1957: "I've got this beautiful young lady and she needs some arrangements. Can you write them?" At the time I was anxious to do any kind of work and see what it sounded like. So I wrote for eight pieces and assembled the band for rehearsals. I wanted Eric to play with the band. I was helping him as much as possible, because I knew he could play well. So I had him on baritone.

Calvin was very impressed with Eric; he had never heard him before. He read the parts and he had such a big, gutsy sound. Merle definitely made sure that the baritone was rattling and the mouthpiece was great. So Calvin said, "Man, this baritone player is great!" Calvin was also doing the Gershwin *Rhapsody in Blue* for about a thirty-piece group. He said, "I want this kid to do the baritone and bass clarinet." And he did, and did a good job. The only thing was that Eric was laughing all evening. When he arrived, I said, "Uh-oh, that's a different Eric." He might have had a little something that night, maybe smoking a bit – I don't know – but he played well. Like I said, it was a period when he was practicing all the time and it was almost getting dangerous, because you can't do that. Then your life is the instrument and no work. When I sent him to New York, it was a very healthy thing. But he was one of the best readers on the date that night, and on baritone and bass clarinet.

In LA, Eric was practicing hard, sounding good, and making a gig one day a week. In the early fifties they had jam sessions every weekend at places like Normandie Hall, with Eric and Ornette

Coleman. Walter Benton and a bunch of the young players, who we met through that period, used to go there and jam every Friday or Saturday night. Eric and Ornette were just two players. We didn't know that they'd get as good as they did and no one else knew. We thought they were just a couple of guys that got on the stand and were trying to find the changes. But I think Eric was probably the more schooled, the one who was more serious about being a complete musician than Ornette, who developed later on, more and more.

Ornette Coleman didn't seem to have his horn together. He had a beard and hair all over his face; sort of looked like a dog. At the jam sessions he might get overlooked because of his appearance and his playing was not conventional at all. He'd be trying, almost screaming on notes, and it didn't necessarily fit the chord. He was always a guy who would try something different. He didn't feel like he wasn't playing. Some people might say, "Oh, I didn't play the right chord on the bridge." But Ornette was there to express his feelings and he had an audience there. I heard he went to one teacher who said, "We'll have to do something with your tone."

Ornette said, "No, I don't want to change that. I don't want to sound like every other saxophone player. I've got my own thing."

He knew where he was going all the time and wasn't interested in being a studio or section player. He had these sounds in his head that he wanted to explore. He was very talented and was trying to do quarter tones on his horn. A little later on, when his group got together with Don Cherry and a few people, the tunes were, at first, a little strange. Even the intonation was weird. But they began to make some of us believe that they knew where they were going.

The unfortunate thing is that there might be some Eric Dolphys and Ornettes around today, but they don't have much chance to have jam sessions. The scene has changed so much. That period allowed those players to develop. There was so much around that they could draw from. Lloyd Reese was here; a bunch of us, who were a little older, were around. We all had something to say and would also be at the jam sessions. Everybody was drawing from each other and that's what allows this talent to come through. The setting was very conducive for those people who wanted to go further, like Eric and

Ornette. Now Eric's gone, but Ornette is right in the prime of a good period, drawing from all those experiences.

It takes a lot to do what Ornette did. I think one time Mingus said that he liked him because he was sincere, even though a lot of people were putting him down, saying, "He's not a musician." "He's no Bird." "He's no this." At one period he just stopped playing and got a job operating an elevator for about six months or a year, because they were shooting at him. But he didn't quit.

Today the picture is so different. People go out socially once a month. It used to be two or three times a week. The price was right and the musicians were playing. Now it's harder to inspire or to develop this kind of talent. There's still a lot of creative talent. I run into them at schools and various places. You see it, but the end results are different. The money is elsewhere. Here in LA, Ben Webster, the great Ben Webster, had to live with his mother, because there was very little work. It's in the studios or getting into the electronics. So there's not much time to just go out and jam, to search for those different notes. We may not see that kind of creativity very much, since it doesn't pay off anymore. There have been a few people from here who have done well recently, like John Carter and Bobby Bradford, but they both had school positions, which guaranteed them rent money. They can get in and be as strange as they want. Maybe they've only got thirty people in the audience, but it can be good. So there's a way to make it now, but not on the basis of your new music and someone coming in with a checkbook and saying, "What do you guys want?" It doesn't happen anymore.

Eric, Ornette, and Charles Lloyd had to go to New York and it was a good time to leave. They weren't completely set and they still had a chance to grow and be discovered on that end, which was great. When you walked in and could play, it didn't take long for it to happen. In Los Angeles you could walk in and play, and still there was no one listening. I think we all suffered from that, knowing that the writers, the critics, didn't write too much about the hometown people. If they did, it wasn't at a time when it helped very much. In New York, whether it was the *Village Voice* or some other papers, they'd do a whole thing on you, tell the people how great you are and where you're going to be playing. We never had that around here, that boosting of the talent. In New York they had people writing in magazines and papers that were devoted to that artistic part of the business, the arts and jazz, and those people did a much better job than out here.

East coasting

In Los Angeles, in the 1950s, Eric was almost going crazy practicing. He sounded good, but nothing was happening for him. He was getting known, but just locally. Since he was staying at home, he didn't need a lot of money and his whole life was one horn to the other ... until Chico Hamilton called me one day. Chico, not Charles Mingus. Although Eric would later play with Mingus, and although they knew each other in Los Angeles, they had never played together out here. So when Chico Hamilton called around 1957, and wanted me to come to New York, I said, "I've got a guy for you." I knew it would do wonders for him. "Get out of here! Out of LA!"

Very few could make it here, very few have. They've all left. Chico said a couple of years ago that I was the only one who made it here. Of course, there is also Gerald Wiggins, Harold Land and Teddy Edwards. Even though Teddy spends a lot of time in Europe, he's not nearly as big as he would have been, if he had been in New York. Jackie Kelson is one of the most underrated players around. He is an excellent clarinet player, one of the very best, but isn't given enough of a chance to play it. I think he doesn't know how good he is on it, although now many are beginning to discover how good he is. What does a great player like Kelson have to do to get the recognition he deserves? Probably have to make a record, laying out his own money to finance it. The critics and others should give this talent more recognition. This is why a lot of musicians go to Europe or to New York, where they get the attention they deserve. Los Angeles won't allow them to get that recognition.

When Eric went with Chico, he took his bass clarinet and he started utilizing everything. After a month or two he called me back and said, "Man, why do you stay there? You can get anything you want here. This is where they want you. They're looking for you." I would have liked to, but I was raising my daughters then and really couldn't leave. It did him a lot of good to get to New York and find that he was well liked. Coleman Hawkins heard him and said, "Man, I don't know where you come from, but that's the kind of sound that we used to hear on the alto."

While I was in New York in 1963 and staying at Charles Lloyd's apartment (I got Charles the job with Chico), Eric used to come by every day and we'd talk. I'd have breakfast, a little cereal; we'd play duets for about three hours; then we'd go to lunch, although Eric wasn't eating lunch. He told me that he and John Coltrane were on health food pills and honey, two or three tablespoons of honey. I didn't think that sounded too good, but they felt it made them much stronger when they played. He and Trane would say, "Gosh, we're playing longer than ever," and they really were. It must have been all that sugar giving them great energy. We'd practice all the time and when I wanted to buy him a meal, he'd just say no. He had the pills and the honey, and he figured that was going to do it. I never saw him eat any solid foods over that six weeks.

The only time I'm aware of, when Eric was unhappy back east, was one time when he recorded with Coltrane. The session lasted all night; I got a call from him afterwards. It was about 6 a.m. and he was in tears.

"I had to talk to somebody. I'm so hurt. Trane played the whole tape off." In other words, Trane must have played thirty choruses. "Finally the engineer said, 'We have more than enough for a couple of albums.'" He never got to play and was frustrated.

I just said, "Well, look, that's going to happen, but your turn will come."

While I was in New York, Eric got a loft. He came by and asked me to take a look. He picked me up in his Volkswagen bug and drove me around to it. It was like a big dance studio, one open space and it was huge. He wanted the loft mainly so he could practice late at night. He still needed to get a couple of hundred bucks. I said, "Shoot, I've got money." He said no, there's a guy in New York, a

Mr. Martin or Kramer, or whatever, who liked to help artists. So I went with him to phone.

"This is Eric Dolphy and someone told me to call you about getting a loan for $400."

It was all so positive and the guy said, "Yeah, okay, I know who you are, so get it back to me whenever it's feasible for you."

He got it and didn't need a penny from me. A musician's story . . . kind of nice.

A year later, during a tour of Europe with Mingus' band in the spring of 1964, Eric decided to stay in Europe because he was so well accepted over there. Mingus told me that when they got off the plane in Germany, the people were shouting, "Eric! Eric!" He was even better received than Mingus. Eric loved New York, but no one really could resist the acclaim he got in Europe. While performing in Germany that summer, he passed out on stage, went into a coma, and died a few days later. Mingus kept saying, "The Germans poisoned him. Why would he just fall out like that, when he was so great?" It was an ugly thing for a while. The autopsy revealed that he was a diabetic, which he didn't know. His parents weren't aware of that either. When I talked to his father after he died, he was so puzzled. I asked his dad, "They said he was a diabetic. Were you aware that he was doing the honey and stuff?"

"No, we weren't."

Maybe those eating habits really hurt him. Eric was riding on top of the world, and for it to happen like that. . . . It was a hard one.

We helped Eric's parents bring him home. Gerald Wilson and I organized a big benefit at Basin Street at Western Avenue and Pico Boulevard to raise some money to cover the expenses. Everyone turned out; it was some day. But it was a sad moment when they shipped the body back to Los Angeles. Eric's dad told me that when he went down to the airport, they had the box sealed and wouldn't open it.

"Well, it's probably not my son then," because his dad couldn't see the body. He just went wild on them: "I don't know that's my son. You're just showing me a box!" The more he told the story, you could see what frame of mind he was in.

"You've got to sign this," they said.

"I'm not doing anything. You haven't proved to me that's my son. You're showing me a box."

They didn't want to do it, but he went on like that until they finally cranked it open. "Okay, he's my son, so let me sign the papers." That was such a blow to Eric's parents. You never get over a thing like that. He'd never given them any trouble that I know of, and all of a sudden it just. . . . So it was a tough one.

Mingus made quite a scene at the funeral. He was raving, saying someone had poisoned Eric in Europe. I picked him up at the airport, drove to the funeral with him, and he was just like a wild animal. He was so distraught, he jumped into the grave yelling, "They killed Eric! I don't want to live." We had to pull him out. Whatever it was that caused Eric's death, whether or not it was something to do with the diet and honey, it's still a mystery.

9
Lives tinged with sadness

Bands and Southern tours

During the late 1940s I began to work with Benny Carter, who I had met about the time of the Stars of Swing job. Lucky Thompson took me to Benny's house and that was an experience. There he was with all this food; he had a great appetite at the time. Benny Carter, Oscar Peterson, and Ray Brown. Those guys would sit together and see who could outeat each other! When Lucky and I arrived, Benny said, "You guys hungry?"

We said, "No."

"Well, I'm a little hungry."

And he reached into the refrigerator, pulled out these collard greens from the night before, about half a dozen eggs, a big piece of ham, two or three pieces of toast, and probably some rice. It was almost like a Thanksgiving dinner, and Benny ate every bit of it. Naturally, I had been impressed with his musical ability, but I didn't know about this side of him.

After I knew Benny a little better, he hired me for his band. He knew of me and he also knew that I had studied with Merle Johnston. Merle always used to rave about his best students. He was the kind of guy who would pick up the phone and say, "Benny, one of my guys you've got to hire, Buddy Collette. He's really one of the best guys." Eventually both Bill Green and I got calls from Benny. We both played altos in his band during the late 1940s at places like the Hollywood Palladium. He was impressed with us because we could read and we were up-and-coming players.

I didn't play much tenor then; occasionally I'd borrow one for a record date or something like that. I had to borrow a tenor when

Wilbur Baranco was in town. He came down to do some Army-Air Force-type shows, some recordings with an all-star band, including Lucky Thompson, Britt Woodman and Eugene Porter. This one day in particular, I got a call at the last minute, two o'clock. He was ready to start and Lucky hadn't shown up yet. Lucky would always come late and Baranco was tired of that. It was only about fifteen minutes from my house; I lived on Forty-seventh Street. I got there about twenty after two and Lucky at about quarter to three. He lost the job and was pretty unhappy.

"Well, look, man, I had car trouble," he said.

"But you've done this to us many times."

So I played tenor. That went on and on until, finally, I was playing tenor regularly.

Later on I was with Herb Geller, who was a fine saxophonist, and his wife, pianist Lorraine Geller. They had a job down on Main Street. It was two saxes and a rhythm section, and they broadcast one night a week. It was better for me to play tenor than alto, because Herb was playing alto then. At that time I was probably playing more like Coleman Hawkins or Ben Webster, sort of a big sound, but on ballads I was influenced more by Lester Young. I would lean towards singing more. We had a good band, were on the radio, and I had some nice solos.

One night, about half an hour after the radio broadcast, I looked up and there's Benny Carter and a couple of other guys walking in.

"Hey, Benny, what are you doing here?"

"I heard a tenor player on the radio and I had to come down to see who that was." I started laughing, because he couldn't know who it was. He'd never heard me on tenor, but he was impressed. "That was a tenor player! I didn't know who could be in town playing like that!"

That's an incident that lets you know what this whole thing's about: What does it sound like? And Benny was judging it basically on that. "This guy's somebody that I've got to know." If there's one thing that I've learned about Benny, it's that if there's something going on, he'll come and check it out in person. They were supposed to be having dinner at the time, listening to the radio, and Benny said, "Let's go down and see who that is." There weren't any freeways, so they had to take surface streets from the Hollywood Hills to Main Street in downtown Los Angeles. That was a nice little trip then.

I also went on the road with Joe Liggins's rhythm and blues band playing alto and baritone. We went down south in 1947, '48. I never thought I'd work with Joe Liggins. I wasn't too impressed with him as a bandleader, but I knew he'd had a hit with "The Honeydripper." We both lived out in the Compton area then, and one day he said, "Buddy, I need a baritone player and one who plays alto. Can you suggest somebody? Get back to me, will you?" I didn't find anyone and I didn't get back to him. About three or four days before he left, he called me. I still didn't have a player for him. I began to think about it. I wasn't working that much and I'd never been South either, so I thought, "Why don't I just take it."

It was a great trip, seeing what the South was at that time, but it was tough. It really was tough, because I had never seen the prejudice so strong. We'd stop in gas stations to go to the bathroom and be told, "Just go out there in the field, son." You couldn't go into most restaurants; there'd be guards around the water fountains and there were no hotels for you. You'd have to go on the other side of the tracks, the black side of town. Sometimes you'd play on the white side, but you'd have to come in through the back door and stay back there during intermissions. So I really felt it, especially coming from Los Angeles, which was not great by any means, but it was so much better. You suddenly realized that all the stories that you'd heard were true.

We got good treatment from blacks. They would take us into their homes, and cook meals for us that you would not believe: biscuits and honey and pies, just great home-cooked stuff. They treated us like kings. So you had two things. There were times when we were nothing in a way, and other times when, "We just want you to sleep in our bed." I'd never seen that before. If they loved your music, they would come out and really treat you well. I'm glad I took that trip. It was an eye-opener, a period of learning.

There were also times when we had a lot of job cancellations. Once we were in Richmond, Virginia, and didn't have jobs for the next week. They were all cancelled. I sent home for money and at that time it could take three days. So James Jackson, the tenor player at the time, and I had about five dollars apiece in our pockets and no job for about a week. We were broke and I'd never had that experience. We'd go to the show for twenty cents or so; watch cowboy movies; eat hot dogs and drink sodas, stalling for those three or four days until the money came in. It was a great experience finding out what the road was about.

I also did a southern trip with Eddie "Rochester" Anderson. He used to work with Jack Benny. People knew him because of television and radio, and his show was called "The Eddie 'Rochester' Anderson Show." They chartered a big bus and we took off. Again, the experience of the South was rough and tough. There was a guy and his wife, a dance team from Nigeria, in the show. Because they had the accent, they could go in places that a lot of us couldn't, just because the southern whites knew they weren't U.S. blacks. The accent would really throw them. It was amazing.

Raising my family

By the early 1950s I was meeting a lot of people, getting busier and becoming known. I was having an exciting, successful career for a young guy of about thirty. It was happening! What else could you say? Brand new car, family's doing good. At this point I had one daughter, Cheryl Ann; my son, William Zan, was about seven years old. Another daughter, Veda Louise, was born around 1954, and my last, Crystal, was born in 1967. Crystal was born after we divorced and I don't think Louise even knew who the father was. But she's still my daughter and I have four children.

However, by the early fifties we were hassling at home. Louise was an alcoholic and drinking most of the time. She had been a dancer at the Club Alabam and Lincoln Theatre, and then her opportunities stopped. When Central Avenue fell off, there wasn't

100

much work for chorus-line dancers. There was not a lot of money coming in and why have a whole line, when you could get away with maybe an entertainer and one singer or something like that, a small combo rather than a big band. It got to the point where she was drinking all the time, and there were periods when we separated.

I knew before we got married that Lou drank a little bit, just loved a taste. It didn't seem like a terrible thing. During our first five years of marriage, we had bought a house and started a family. Everything seemed like it would fall into place. Then it got to be a real habit of drinking every day and at all times of the day, and another side started coming out. There seemed to be nothing else but booze. She liked it whenever her friends would come over at noon and put a jug on the table. Often I'd be on my way to school or practicing in the back room, when she'd wander in to tell me that I sounded better years ago. She didn't have any understanding of practicing, scales and long tones. More and more the relationship crumbled. Once she threw my horn out the door and bent it all up. She was jealous of it.

Finally, I couldn't take any more and went to stay at my grandmother's one night. When I came back, Lou didn't say much. A few months later, I told her I was going to leave. I'd figured out that we weren't going to make it. All she said was that since I was leaving, could I stop by the store, bring her back a pint, and put it on the doorstep. I told her no and left.

I moved into an apartment on St. Andrew's Place with Jimmy Cheatham and John "Streamline" Ewing. They had found a place with three bedrooms and three baths, and must have known what I was going through. They approached me reluctantly, saying, "We have this apartment and we can't handle it by ourselves." It only cost about $275 a month at that time. I said, "Fine." I didn't move out right away, but I began to have some peace of mind when I needed it. Eventually we separated for about four or five years.

I never saw Lou, but I'd try to see the kids on weekends. Lou was becoming such a bad influence. She kept her drinking routine and had continuous parties with the wrong people. Many times she'd be passed out, lying on the floor. It was just a terrible situation. After a few years Lou started talking a little better, so we decided to try it again. Even though we had Cheryl, it didn't work out and we broke up again. The pattern was still there. It only took a week or two for it to surface. It was hard bringing up kids in that atmosphere. We finally divorced.

Lou retained custody, but that situation wasn't good, and, finally, I had to get them away from her legally. Sometimes the kids would call me from school and tell me that she hadn't been there in three days. Lou would be drinking. It was so terrible. She kept drinking until she was put in a mental hospital and that happened a few times. She got so thin and her face was like a mask. I was in and out of there all the time trying to help. We had two daughters by then. I'd go out there and buy them some food, encourage them, and tell them that while there wasn't much I could do now, I promised to put things right.

My lawyer, Leo Branton, told me that all we could do was keep an eye on them, and at the first opportunity move in and try to take the kids. When that time came, we set up a court date and went in with our fingers crossed, because Lou had a habit of bouncing back. At that time it was difficult for the father to get custody. The court date was for 9 a.m. at the downtown courthouse, and everyone was there except Lou. After ten minutes the judge asked if anyone knew where Mrs. Collette was. No one did. At nine-thirty the judge, disgusted, called us up again. "Well, I don't know what kind of lady this is, but she's not here. The girls are ten and eight. Can you raise these young ladies?" I said that I could do pretty well. Then he said that since I felt I could, he'd grant me legal custody.

My daughters Cheryl Ann and Veda Louise came to live with me, and my son was about seventeen when he came to live with us. Crystal came when she was about fifteen. It's harder to instill the right values, but they all did fine.

My marriage with Lou was a life experience and it often comes out in my music, nothing bitter or ugly, but more tinged with a little sadness sometimes. You can go right to the mood and reflect on it;

you're putting the feeling in there. You've experienced it; you know those moments.

As a father I really experienced a good part of life, which I think is very valuable. You've got kids and you have to split your schedule with them, no matter how busy you are as a player. And I was at one of my busiest periods then. I decided this was going to be more important than having my name up on marquees and being a famous musician, and then having kids that are not making it. I just decided that somebody's got to do this. My ex-wife couldn't do it. She was going in and out of the hospital – Metropolitan and Camarillo State Hospitals. Those kids had to make it and are making it now, but it wasn't easy.

Now I'm very wealthy, not in dollars, but the kids are healthy and I've got eight grandkids and three great-grandchildren. I was pretty good on the horns, but I didn't have much time to go out and celebrate my so-called success and my achievements, even though there were a lot of them. But it paid off. I was able to balance being a successful musician – jazz musician, classical musician, teacher – and a father.

Breaking bread with Bird

In the early 1950s, when we had the apartment on St. Andrew's Place with Jimmy and Stream, Gerry Mulligan's group had just started working at the Haig on Wilshire Boulevard near the Ambassador Hotel. Chico Hamilton, their drummer, wanted to know if they could rehearse at our apartment. It was the first time they rehearsed the new Mulligan group without a piano. They had Chet Baker, Chico and Bob Whitlock, who was the first bass player before Carson Smith. The first rehearsal didn't sound too great, because they didn't seem to know how to play without the piano. It was a shifting of gears.

At the Haig it wasn't going that well initially. People weren't too impressed with a group without a piano. Finally, Gerry figured out how to make it work by playing more counter lines on the baritone, while Chet played melody and soloed. When Gerry would be soloing, Chet would do the same thing. There would be a countermelody. They weren't trying to have two solos at once, but just to enhance or reinforce what the soloist was doing. That began to work and they kept it interesting. The main thing was interest, rather than having the piano comping all the chords.

We had many celebrities coming by that apartment all the time. Charlie Parker was there. He was working at a place called the Tiffany Club, which was near the Haig. One thing about Bird; he could pick three other musicians to make his quartet and they could be people who couldn't play well, but when they played with him, he had some magical charm to make them sound great. He had such musical strength in his own playing that the rest of the group would have something to hang on to.

When Bird finished his job at the Tiffany Club one Friday, Streamline, Jimmy and I invited him to dinner on Saturday. We cooked fried chicken and mashed potatoes – the works – and spent most of the afternoon and evening just eating, drinking, talking, and relaxing. He told a lot of great stories. His nickname, he said, went back to when he was about fourteen or fifteen years old in Kansas City – not later on when he was with the McShann band – and had nothing to do with the stories that were being passed around about him eating chicken or picking up a chicken on the road that had been hit by a car. He hated those stories. He told us that he used to get up about four or five in the morning to practice in a nearby park, and would always take at least one friend with him, a drummer or a bassist, or whoever would get up that early. Often they'd get high out there. The cops would drive by and wave at them. They allowed them to practice, as long as it was far enough away from the residential area. That's when the nickname came. The people heard that little alto of his so often in the park that they started calling him "Bird."

He also told us about an event that occurred during one of his trips to Europe. He was the only jazz player invited to this big banquet of about twenty or thirty of the top players in Europe's symphony orchestras. The invitation stated, "You are invited to this banquet dinner and please bring your instrument." There was no rhythm section there and it was clearly not a jam session. There were all guys, no women. They had dinner and then cognac and cigars. At one point the host got up and said, "Would you care to do something for four or five minutes? Just play what you want." They went around the table and each artist performed for a few minutes. He told us how thrilled he was just to hear all that. Bird didn't say what he played, but you know he could do anything. He had almost total recall, even of a lot of the classical material. He'd be playing jazz and then all of a sudden there would be quotes from *Daphnis and Chloe* or *The Firebird Suite*, and it would fit. He must have thrown them. He was given a flute by one of the top European players, a Selmer sterling silver.

I said, "Well, I'd love to hear you play some. I'll get mine, if you want to try it out."

"Don't get it! I'll let you know when I want you to hear me. I'm still working on what I'm working on."

He also talked about his early influences. I asked, "By the way, who did you like when you were coming up?"

"There were two people I was really influenced by: Lester Young and Charlie Christian. I can sing any solo on record that Lester has played."

I knew he was right. If you're going to be a jazz player, Lester paved another way, not just for tenor players, but for music in general, where you're talking with your instrument. You're having a conversation. Bird caught it and that's why he said, "Yeah, he was a main influence."

When I asked him about Charlie Christian, he said, "I wanted my alto to sound like his guitar." And Charlie Christian was marvelous. You could put a lyric to everything he played. In fact, I heard him with Art Tatum. Those were the giants around here at the time. Jimmy Blanton and Charlie died early; Art was around a little longer. But those guys were dynamite players.

We had started about noon and now it was getting to be about seven or eight o'clock. We had been drinking cognac and smoking cigars. We were having fun, just a great day with him being there, getting to know him better and hearing all these stories. Then he

105

began to change a little, began to talk about things he didn't like. We had the radio on and a record was playing. It was "The Hawk Talks," which was written and arranged by Louie Bellson, and recorded by Duke Ellington. As Bird listened, I saw him make a little gesture when it came to the drum solo, and then he asked, "Why did he play that kind of solo there?" I knew what he meant. Everything was going along quite well and all of a sudden there was a Gene Krupa, ratatatata, ratatatata drum solo. That's what bothered him. His taste was almost perfect and that pattern didn't fit the arrangement.

We went on talking and he said that he'd died nine times. You could tell he was miserable with the way his life had turned out: because of the dope, because of not being able to work, and because he was not getting the benefits he thought should have been his, being able to perform as the kind of player he was. He was still getting peanuts. We talked about what Stream, Jimmy and I were doing. Then he finally said, "I wish I could be like you."

I knew what Parker meant. I could tolerate the scene. I was flexible enough. I could hang in there. It would bother him to play those clubs. He'd make $200 a week, but that would be it. No other work, no money, just constant turmoil. Sometimes I'd have to give him dinner money. He'd have to say, "Got a couple of bucks 'til I make the gig on Saturday?" I was happy to do anything to help him, but that felt terrible. I'd make $130 just for one hour of one night in the studio. We were comfortable, had a nice place, nice car, money coming in, on top of the world, although we didn't know it at the time. I was doing the Groucho Marx Show, making enough money to do almost anything I wanted. I had all of my instruments, was getting offers from different bands, including one from Duke Ellington. He called me personally on the phone. "Buddy, this is Edward K. Ellington and I want you to come with the band and feature that flute of yours."

How do you say no to a guy like that? But I hemmed and hawed. I was in school, had Groucho, and things were happening. So I turned him down. If that had happened at any other time, I would have taken it.

106

Right then, Bird made up a little poem, which he told me to write down and which I still have:

My shame is the life
I've lived for so long.
A personal thing is for instance
The longed for years
I shall never live
Are my tears.

Cool is the day.
The wind and the breeze
My head shall clear
Without a sneeze.

A day will come when
I shall smile up.
You shan't see me
But watch the blue buttercup.

ARTBHURD (By Charlie Parker, © 2000 Charlie Parker
Music Co.)

About ten or eleven o'clock, we'd drunk up all the cognac and Bird got hungry again. We went into the kitchen and pulled out the rest of the chicken. He attacked it almost like an animal, angrily tearing off the bones. It's a wonder he didn't chew them. It was interesting to see, because he was very quiet most of the day. Now he was full of cognac and very strong.

Then, about 11.30 p.m, Bird said, "Let's play." He had his alto there. I didn't want him to leave without playing, if he wanted to play. So we got our horns out and he said, "Call your shot," like a pool player.

"Whatever you want," I said.

Once he started, I knew he'd be blowing for an hour or two. He lit into something, started making modulations and all kinds of stuff, impossible for most people to do without a rhythm section. His time was great. He could play, then stop for a bar and a half, and the next phrase would come right in with no time lost. I knew we might get evicted from that apartment, but we had to take the chance. If the eviction notice came, we felt it would have been worth it. We didn't play, because we would have missed too much. It was like a concert from two feet away. That night in the kitchen with Bird just blowing, I heard rhythm sections behind him. He's the only one I've ever heard do that. He played for an hour before he put it away. Then we gathered up his stuff and I took him back to the hotel.

He had to express, get things out of his system, all the stories through the years, beginning with Jay McShann. He told me that when he was with McShann's band, he could never quite get enough playing in. He'd have his solo, but when someone else was playing, he'd walk outside in the Kansas City snow in whatever he'd have on and practice to the sound of the band coming from inside. He built that sound of his by playing outside in the snow, in the park as a kid, and then later with McShann. It's very difficult to move your hands outside in the cold, but that's what he'd go out and do.

When he lived in Los Angeles, he couldn't play in his apartment, so he blew in South Park at Fifty-second Street and San Pedro. He'd go out there, take a little nap. Maybe he'd been up all night. Then he'd take the alto out and play. Most people around the park didn't know who he was or what he was playing. Most people in LA then didn't know how great he was.

Throughout the years, thinking about Charlie Parker, there were so many marvelous moments and he influenced us in so many different ways. There was a great jam session at Jack's Basket Room after Bird came out of Camarillo State Hospital. He had been quite ill, having problems with drugs and going through other things. It was the night he'd been released. There was an annouce-ment that he was going to come and jam. When he arrived, he looked great, really sharp, as healthy as anybody could, and this was his night. I hadn't ever seen him like that before. There must have been thirty or forty different musicians all wanting to show Parker how they could play. All the tenor and alto players were there – Sonny Criss, Wardell Gray, Dexter Gordon, Gene Phillips, Teddy Edwards, Jay McNeely, and on and on. They all played and Bird just sat there and smiled. It was a long night. Finally, Bird got up there and I don't think he played more than three or four choruses. But he told a complete story, caught all the nuances, tapered off to the end. Nobody played a note after that. Everybody just packed up their horns and went on home, because it was so complete, so right.

Looking back, he wasn't a man of many words, but his words were like his music. People think of him as having many notes, but not really. When you analyze Parker, there's a gem here, a bridge, another gem. Bird was editing properly in his playing at certain points. He could play fast and that's why a lot of players, as much as they try to sound like him or get close to his licks, always play more than he does. The mistake players are making now is too many notes, too many gems everywhere, like a kid with too many toys at Christmas. They get confused. With your best compositions all you need is a little theme here, a little frill, a little icing. That's probably why those European classical players invited him to dinner, because of his mind, his concept and form of music. He studied, but at the same time had total recall and perfect pitch, all those gifts came together. The music that he left, you could be drawing from for years and years, and still never get it all. There it is in a bar or two, enough to last a long time, while a lot of players just play, play, play, play. They've got a million ideas, but it's not fresh. It's tired, just something borrowed from someone else.

This music started a bunch of us thinking that there was more to do using notes other than those from the basic chords and scales. That's when even the twelve-tone system began to come in. Of course, Schoenberg and people like that were doing it in European classical music, but in jazz, Lyle "Spud" Murphy has the equal interval system that he's been teaching. Oscar Peterson and Gerry Wiggins studied with him, and I studied with him. The Schillinger system is a twelve-tone system. Later I also studied with a guy named George Trembley, who more or less derived his own twelve-tone system. Bird's music opened us up.

10

The amalgamation of Local 767 and Local 47

I had been a member of the musicians' union since I was sixteen or seventeen. The black local, 767, was on Central Avenue at Seventeenth Street and the white local, 47, was on Georgia Street, near Figueroa. Local 47 moved to its current location on Vine Street in Hollywood in 1947 or 1948. It was a fabulous building and it was really stunning to see a union like that. Of course, we knew about it, but hadn't visited it, because it was only for whites. You could walk in if you wanted, but they'd say, "Who are you looking for? You have to go over to the other union." In the Hollywood area, there were very few blacks ever in the restaurants or around the area. If you saw a black there in those days, they would either be going to or getting off from work somewhere, and not socializing.

When I was in the navy, they were trying to integrate the services. But even at the base where we were in northern California, it was an all-black band and the cadets were all white. At that time it didn't bother us, because that's the way life was. When I got back home, I started thinking this should not be, that it would also hinder our future development because of the things we were stuck with: our old union building on Central Avenue, where the foundation of the building was uneven and the pianos were out of tune. It would also prevent togetherness on all levels for black and white musicians, who were working together. When I first started on the Groucho Marx show, Ben Barrett was the contractor and would pay everybody their checks, then collect the work dues from all the guys, which was about two dollars and fifty cents a week. He would come to me and say, "I want two-fifty – Oh! You're at the other union. I only need a dollar-fifty from you."

And the guys would say, "What do you mean? He's paying less than we are?"

My line was, "Well, there are a lot of things that are going to be that way, as long as we are on separate sides of town."

I knew that somehow they were going to play us against each other and they did.

We thought about it, especially those of us who had been in the service, and Mingus, who hadn't been in the military. We kept thinking, "Man, we'll never make it with two unions, because we're getting the leftovers." All the calls came to Local 47. Now and then they might want a black band for a sideline call, where the music had been recorded by the white band and they wanted to show a black group. We'd all jump on it, of course, because it was more money than you could make in a club. For a day you'd make fifty dollars and in a club you could probably only make about ten dollars.

So it was a good day, except you had to get up at about five in the morning to be at the studio at eight and they might use you until four. You'd be on call all day. If you'd go to sleep, which a lot of us would do, you'd hide out in a corner. If you were caught, they'd be on you. It was good financially, but not the best treatment. Some days you might even wind up making $100. That was a lot of money, but that may not happen for another year or two.

At Local 47 that was happening all the time. I knew it was, because I was around those guys. I'd go to *The Jack Smith Show* with Barney Kessel and some guys at other shows. They'd be doing this kind of thing all the time, working radio shows and pulling down $200 or $300 a week. That wasn't going to get better for us with the two unions and that was a real shaft.

The Community Symphony Orchestra

I'll give Mingus credit for the actual beginning of the struggle to end this segregation. He was always fighting the battle of the racial situation. In 1949, he got a job with Billy Eckstine at the Million Dollar Theatre on Broadway. Mingus was the only non-white in the band. I don't know if they realized he was black. Because he was very light-skinned, I guess a lot of people thought he might have been Mexican more than black. Since Billy Eckstine was a black leader, Mingus figured, "Why couldn't there be a few blacks in there?" Mingus was the only one and he let them know that he didn't like it. And he could be tough on you; everybody in the band had to hear it every day: "You guys are prejudiced! You should have some more blacks. You could hire Buddy Collette." My name was being tossed around so much that the guys hated me without knowing me!

I'd see Mingus at the end of the evening. He would always check with me every day. "Man, those guys don't think you can play. They could have hired some more blacks in the band and I told them about it. There's one flute player down there who plays good. He said he wouldn't mind you coming down, and you guys could play some duets to see who's the best." I was finally invited down and I was curious about the band. We wanted to meet people that understood what we were talking about: the unions getting together, people getting together, stopping all this. Mingus said, "Okay, he wants you to come down on Thursday. Come to the show with me and in between shows you guys can play duets. You can get to know him." The guy's name was Julie Kinsler. I didn't know any of the guys in the band at the time. I think I'd seen Tommy Peterson, who was a trombone player and the leader, but he was hard to get to know. He was a nice guy and a great player, but so much into himself.

I got there, saw the show, then went to the back room with my flute. Julie said, "Oh, I've heard a lot about you. Mingus says you're a good flute player." He had his duets, a nice Kuhlau book of duets, and a few other things. He was very studious, a good player, and a nice man. So I said, "Whatever you've got, we can play." Mingus sat there watching. Everybody else had gone for food. They didn't care about it. I mean they were nice enough, but were just, "Hey! See you. Take care." We played duets for an hour. Mingus never realized – and when I told him later, he didn't believe it – that Julie pulled out duet books that I had at home. I never told the guy. Most flute players in town were studying with Marty Ruderman or somebody like that. They all wanted you to have those Kuhlau books. When he pulled them out, I kind of smiled. I probably could have sightread it, but I had been working on those things a little bit.

Julie kept saying, "My! Two years?" I kind of smiled. We got to be good friends, because he really appreciated it. "Man, you're going to do all right."

Then we said, "What we are trying to do is get the unions together."

"I'd like that, too, but talk to Milt Holland," who was the drummer.

I waited for Milt to come back from lunch and approached him. Milt said, "Man, we've been wanting to do this, too. I know about six or eight people that think just the way you guys do. We can get together and start meetings or something." Mingus and I lit up, because that was the first time we heard anybody who was really excited about it.

As Mingus and I were going home that night he said, "Man, you got him! You played better than he did."

"No. He pulled out duets that I knew."

"Oh, man, you didn't have those duets. You just read everything in sight." Mingus just wanted to say that we got him.

The next day Mingus and I met with a few of the guys who felt the same way and wanted to call a big meeting. I said, "Well, I don't think we should call a meeting, because the guys that I know don't like meetings too much." Instead, most of us had been studying for a few years and I said that we needed a situation where we could learn the music, possibly like a symphony rehearsal orchestra. "The thing that most of the blacks and minorities might need at this point would be a training ground, a training period." The more I'd see of studio work, hanging out with guys like Barney Kessel, the more I knew that a lot of guys would be lacking in the training. It might have taken them four or five years. But if there was some rehearsal band, then they would learn.

Milt said, "If that's what you want, that's easy. I know all the people from that world."

That was the beginning of the Community Symphony Orchestra.

Our main goal was to make sure more blacks were placed in different circuits, because at that time we only worked clubs. If we did play the Orpheum Theatre or the Million Dollar, it was in a black band or when an all-black show would be there. For the other shows, if they'd need twenty musicians, blacks wouldn't get the call at all, no matter how good you were. It just didn't happen. So that was the idea: can we show that it can work?

Milt said, "Okay, get as many people as you can, then we'll fill in." Milt was beautiful, is still beautiful.

So I got Bill Green, me, Britt Woodman, Jimmy Cheatham, John Ewing, Red Callender, and another young man who played oboe, James McCullough. That wasn't a big number, but those were some of the people that were going in the right direction, who had enough study behind them to take advantage of this, and who were interested in playing this kind of music. Mingus wasn't there. He didn't want to do symphony music; he always wanted to do his own material. He was with us politically, but musically it wasn't his world.

We scheduled a rehearsal and the excitement started mounting. We were on the phones talking to people and many of them just wanted to be there: "Interracial symphony? Let's do that!" We got the top clarinetists and flutists in town, including Arthur Cleghorn, who joined us later on and was one of the finest flutists. Joe Egger was a great French horn player. John Graas was classical and into jazz on the french horn. A lot of enthusiasm. Some would approach our rehearsal like it was one they were getting paid for downtown. We had something like five flutists, when you only needed three. They just wanted to be there. In no time the Orchestra had grown to about sixty-five pieces.

We had a board to set policy and to let people know about the Orchestra. The main aim was to bring about one musicians' union in Los Angeles, black and white under the same roof. Some of the whites even came over and tried to get in our union, but they were told, "You can't do it." We were trying different things. We also had a black woman, Thelma Walker, a very articulate woman, who wanted to help out. She would always state our policy at the rehearsals: "This is the Community Symphony Orchestra and it's organized to help the minorities know more about symphony music. We appreciate anyone coming, but this is something that's necessary, where we can have more togetherness, because our main goal is to have one union where everyone can work together in the studios and clubs, and everywhere."

The Orchestra rehearsed at Humanist Hall, Twenty-third and Union, and then we moved every now and then to Hollywood at Le Conte Junior High School near Sunset and Gower. We were just rehearsing, but people would come. The first night we had a conductor who was world renowned – Eisler Solomon. He happened to be in town for a week or so. Joe Egger or someone in the Orchestra asked him, "How would you like to conduct an interracial orchestra?"

And he said, "When? I would love to do it." He was excited, he really was.

That got us in the papers; the press was there snapping pictures like crazy. People were really buzzing. That first night we had a black bass player named Henry Lewis. He was playing so well he sounded like three basses. A very fine talent, he was only about nineteen years old then. Later on he became a famous conductor; conducted in Los Angeles for a while, and married an opera singer, Marilyn Horne. We had other great conductors, too: Peter Cohen, Dr. Al Sendry, Dr. Walker.

At one of the meetings I asked, "Why don't we have a black conductor? There's a guy that's qualified, and he's here." So Percy McDavid led the orchestra one night. He was a wonderful musician and teacher. He was one of Bill Green's teachers, when Bill was in Kansas City. McDavid also had taught Illinois and Russell Jacquet, Arnett Cobb, Maurice and Freddie Simon. He had so many students. Percy was a fine pianist and teacher, taught in the public schools, and was into classical music as well.

Then someone said, "We're doing okay on the classical. Why don't we have a jam session for the jazz and we can also get more people who aren't in tune with jazz to understand the music." So we had Monday night for classical and then Sunday afternoon for jazz, and we'd invite the classical people. The Sunday event built up fast and we had great jam sessions.

One time we got ahold of trumpeter Harry "Sweets" Edison, who was working with Josephine Baker. We wanted to get her and some other names to appear on one of the Sunday afternoon sessions. She didn't have to perform, just come out publicly in support of us. She was playing the RKO theater downtown and agreed to come between shows. That day at Humanist Hall we exceeded the limit. The place would hold about two hundred people; we had about five hundred in there.

When Josephine got on stage, she said, "I wonder why you have two unions," something to that effect. "Well, I think it should be one and I don't know why you people are wasting time. You've got all these beautiful people here." She started talking about how there's coming a time when people can work together. Bang! Zing! Finally, she looked down in the audience and there were two little girls, one black and one white, and they're about five years old. She knew when you've got something to work, right? "You and you, come up here." And they both danced up on the stage, where she whispered to them. They grabbed each other, hugged, and wouldn't let go. Josephine looked at the audience and winked, "These kids will show you how to do it," and walked out. And the crowd was . . . great! That was our biggest crowd and it inspired us.

Later on we got Nat King Cole. He was great and did the same thing for us. We got the Club Alabam for a benefit and had all the people in the world. Frank Sinatra didn't do a concert for us, but he sent a statement saying, "There should be one union."

Amalgamation politics

We were building an organization. From contributions and the benefits we'd get money for mailings and notified people. Marl Young, and then Benny Carter, came to help us. We had about three years of hard work and socializing before a lot of the guys came in. Most of it was rehearsals and the jam sessions, and many meetings. We contacted James C. Petrillo, president of the American Federation of Musicians, who didn't like the idea: "I don't see why you have to get together."

We circulated petitions, asking musicians to endorse the idea of amalgamating the two locals. We figured that if we got a thousand musicians saying, "We want amalgamation," it would get things moving. Gerald Wilson, Red Callender, and I went to Los Angeles City College to get petitions signed. We started mainly with Charles Mingus and Britt Woodman, but now it was getting bigger. Gerald and Red were into it. We knew that Buddy Baker was rehearsing at LACC and there were no blacks in his band – not anybody's fault. We wanted to help change that. The three of us knew and loved all the guys there, such as Abe Most, Glenn Johnston, and Jack Dumont. It was a woodwind and brass ensemble. They rehearsed every Tuesday night, since some of those guys were so busy in the studios during the day.

The reaction was more against than for it: "Well, I don't see why we have to sign anything. I'm not interested." They weren't into it and didn't want to get into it. We were strangers in this setting, although we had two or three friends who said, "Well, I'll sign it because I think it's a good idea." They invited Red to play, because he was a famous bass player, and he played that night. There might have been thirty musicians. Most were quite pleasant, but they didn't want to rush into anything. About four or five signed, and there were about three or four who were very frank in saying, "I don't sign anything like that." Who knows what their real reasons were. Later, Glenn Johnston and I got to be pretty close friends. In fact, Bill Green used to be very close to Glenn. He'd be with him practically every day. I don't know how that relationship got started, maybe just with playing together or fixing mouthpieces. Glenn was always an interesting guy, very knowledgeable and everything, but he was also a very opinionated man. I think his first reaction was, "I don't need this!"

It was difficult to approach a lot of people who might say, "I don't," and that happened in both cases, not just with the whites. There were blacks who said, "We don't want this. Why do we want to go and give up what we have?" Our point was that our local didn't have very much, especially the way the union was being operated. Very little money came into the black union and if any jobs came our way from whites, they had to go through the white union first.

The more we pushed, the more we began to pick up people. Later on a lot of white musicians changed their minds. That's the way people are. We found out that a lot of them didn't know there were two unions. For many musicians there was no reason to go down to the union. They used to mail your checks out to you in most cases. When I did the Groucho Marx show, the contractor would have the checks there.

At this point we had all the publicity and people were doing fine, but we still didn't know how to go beyond that. We'd hit a road-block. Finally, we realized the next thing would be electing officers to our local leadership to move it ahead. Our officers in 767 were opposed to it. We didn't have that much, but they thought at least it was still ours. And most of the officers at Local 47 were happy with what they had, of course. They had it great and all the money was coming in there. We decided to set up a slate and run for union office. I ran for president of Local 767. Marl Young, Bill Douglass, and John Anderson ran for other offices. The incumbent, Leo Davis, beat me by about twenty votes out of four hundred. We did win a couple of seats on the Board of Directors, but we still didn't have enough power.

Elections took place every year in our local. So the next year we tried again. We ran Benny Carter for president and he lost to Leo Davis by the same number of votes I did. But this time I ran for the Board and got in; Marl got in; Bill Douglass won the vice president's spot. Now we've got a little power underneath the president, who was a nice man. Marl had studied to be a lawyer, three years of law school, and he loved getting the bylaws and checking everything out. So we were able to move through resolutions and proposals toward a meeting with Local 47. Finally, we got negotiations going.

We had to drag Local 47 into it, because it got to the point of asking why they didn't want it. They were getting more members and we could work together better, but they stalled. Petrillo stalled. A lot of people at 47 stalled. That's why the fight took a long time. When a fight takes a long time like that, of course you're not getting help from all sides. But the more the question was asked, "Is it a racial thing or what is it?" they had to say, "Well, no, it's not that. We just don't know what to call it or how to do it or we can't because it's never been done before and...." So the big stall goes. The unions that were together, like New York Local 802, were that way in the beginning. The others were divided into white and black locals. We were trying something new, but we were also checking out information on how it could be done. Finally, they had no excuse.

It took about three years, but we brought the unions together in April 1953. Looking back, the amalgamation helped a lot of musicians, gave them a better focus or a better picture of what they had to do to look beyond the Central Avenue-type jobs. The ones who really benefited were the ones who wanted to have a successful career in music, rather than just being a leader or somebody who has a record out. It began to make better players out of the good players, and the ones who weren't doing it had to decide to either back away or get serious. If somebody was just doing nightclubs, they were probably doing basically the same. But anybody who wanted to meet with people and experiment with different kinds of music, and do studios and records and be a top craftsperson, then I think they benefited a lot.

There was also better health and welfare, and pension benefits. Now there's health and welfare on your checks. When you do a job, there's pension, which means that after you reach the age of sixty, if you paid pension in all those years, you might have a $1,000- or a $500-a-month check coming to you for life. It wasn't that we weren't doing it well with 767; it's just that it wasn't a big business thing over there. We were just a subsidiary of Local 47. It also allowed some later periods – the 1960s and 1970s – to be very lucrative for a lot of black musicians, who began doing recordings and shows, like *The Carol Burnett Show*, *The Danny Kaye Show*, *The Flip Wilson Show*. Those shows began to hire people because they were in the same union and the word got around who could play, and who couldn't. The other way we were isolated.

It was a great historical step; the first time there was an amalgamation in the musicians' union. Thirty or forty of the locals subsequently followed our method of amalgamating. So the main benefit was a lesson for people that togetherness works. What we found in playing music and being in an artistic field is that color is not very important; it's what people can share with each other. We knew it was time and, looking back, it was one of the best things that could have happened. We thought that something should be done with a human touch to it. Maybe some people will make more money. If not, you can look back at it and say, "We'll never go back to the other way," because we taught a lot of people a lesson, as far as integration is concerned. If we were still separated today, we'd have more problems. It didn't solve all the problems, of course; we've got many of the same problems now. There's still not the fair play that I thought would happen in the studios and TV. I figured that when people got to know each other, they'd get along and say, "Hey, man, you play good. I want to use you in my band." But it was a turning point, a period of hope for everybody, especially for blacks.

So the amalgamation was a step in the right direction. It wasn't designed to solve everything, but we were trying to get people together. Maybe that's the hard thing, because thirty-five years later people still have trouble getting together. But the balance is coming. Now we're a few decades later and they're learning how to respect each other. At the union now we have blacks, women, and Latinos involved in running the Local. It's worked, and people are comfortable with it. We had to show them.

There is something in helping people and being sincere. If you're able to hang in and not worry about it and not use the negative, "They're not hiring me because they don't like me," they've got to learn. What we did and what we are still doing is making sure people can know each other, and want to be the best they can and bounce off of each other's talent. That's what should be happening in the boardroom. So my idea of the amalgamation was to allow people – us – to be what we wanted to be – musicians. We wanted to have every opportunity to grow to the heights, as you can see with Bill Green and many others who did just that.

11
The Jackie Robinson of the networks

"Say the magic word...."

During the amalgamation struggle Jerry Fielding came to one of the rehearsals of the Community Symphony Orchestra. I knew his name because he was a composer and had gotten the job as musical director of the Groucho Marx show, *You Bet Your Life*, as well as *The Life of Riley* show. We were playing Bizet's *Carmen*, and in that piece there's a long flute solo, which I'd never played before. Percy McDavid was conducting and asked, "Buddy, would you like to play the flute solo?" Percy began to conduct and I started playing. The only shocker was when I realized that the whole orchestra wasn't playing; it was only harp and flute for about a minute. It was really a lush spot for anybody. I had gotten confident, was playing better, and was at the point where I had to take a shot. "What's this all about, if I don't finally play something here?" I was nervous. My tone was shaking a little, but I made it through. After the solo the orchestra stopped and the string players tapped their bows on the music stands. That gave me a good feeling: "Wow, they liked me." I knew it wasn't that great, but I didn't falter.

At the end of the evening we were all going home, hugging each other, some going for coffee, and I walked right into Jerry Fielding.

"Pretty good flute you're playing there," he said.

"Oh, thank you. I haven't been playing for too long."

"Do you know Marshal Royal? I've got an opening coming up on the Groucho show."

"I know him, but he just left with Count Basie's orchestra."

"Well, heck, I had a job for him to do. The job was for alto, clarinet, and flute."

"Even if he's here," I told him, "he doesn't play flute yet."

"Well, it's too bad you don't play saxophone."

After he learned I could also play clarinet and saxophone, he hired me on the spot for the Groucho Marx show on the strength of the flute solo. So in 1950 I was the first black to be hired for the studio band at NBC in Hollywood. It was a network show on radio first, then it went to simulcast – TV and radio at the same time. We were just on radio for the first couple of months after I joined the band. The show lasted until 1961.

A week later I met Jerry at Naples Restaurant, which was in back of the studios at CBS, at about four-thirty, an hour and a half before the start of the show. He had my parts and spent about an hour with me going over them. The first time I played the show I wasn't nervous. It was something I had been working for and looking forward to, not just musically, but even meeting the guys and sitting with them. Some of the them, Milt Kestenbaum and Seymour Sheklow, were part of the Community Symphony and that made it great. When I first saw Groucho, he sounded pleased: "We got a new guy in the band!" And he starts screaming, "Hey, how are you doing?" The music didn't bother me, but it was hard. I was like a fighter in top shape; I was ready for a challenge. I knew everything was based on me doing a great job. I couldn't let down. Everything we had been doing with the unions was based on me or someone getting an opportunity and pulling it off. I always thought this was probably how Jackie Robinson felt.

Groucho began to tune into me more. If I was gone, he would come up to the band and say, "Where's Buddy?" He knew me and the guys began to feel: "He knows you and doesn't know us." There were times he would toss out: "We've got a great jazz player here. His name is Buddy Collette." I had won the most valuable clarinet award from *Down Beat* magazine in 1956, and a few other things like that while the show was on. It was a big thing for the leader to go to Groucho and say, "Hey, look who we have in the band!" I'd go to the Monterey Jazz Festival and have the publicity, and he'd love to know that. He'd say, "We've got a jazz guy in the band here," and would throw that on the air at times.

During breaks, five or six of the band would go to dinner. We'd go to restaurants that I could never go to alone, but they accepted it somehow. Later on, sometimes I'd go to those places with someone else, and especially if it was someone white, we'd get the "You can't do this" treatment. We used to go to Nickodell's on Selma, right behind NBC in Hollywood – a very classy place.

Once I went in with a white woman, Nan Evertt, who was a good friend of mine. I had gone there with the players in the band, but not on my own. I was kind of afraid to go in, but Nan said, "Oh, Nickodell's. Great!" She had no idea and she hadn't really had any experience of being refused. In my mind it was a test to see if the two of us could go in and be served.

We opened the door and the maître d' just about lost his teeth. I said, "Two," because I was trying to just outdo him. Stammering, he pointed to the back of the room. The only unfortunate thing about the back was that we had to walk through a crowded, fabulous restaurant. As we passed through, the audience reacted. Spoons fell off the table and it got very noisy for a while. I really got frightened.

The maître d' put us in the back, where everyone could see us. We couldn't hide from anyone. It was a good thing they had large menus. In a way it was a perfect setting. We looked great; I was sharp and she was decked out, but the noises lasted throughout dinner. There was coughing, all kinds of ways of letting you know without coming over and saying, "We don't like you and do not approve of this." It was the most miserable evening. I wanted to keep the menus up in front of our faces the whole time. We made it through dinner, but we were very happy to get out of there. I was getting to know the Hollywood area quite well. But it was very lonely, because most of the time there were no other blacks out there.

The same kind of thing happened again when Jerry Fielding and I went with some friends to see Mingus with Red Norvo and Tal Farlow. They were working on La Cienega Boulevard in a little spot and Jerry wanted to hear some jazz. Milt Kestenbaum, our bass player, Thelma Walker, and Nan Evertt were with us. We went in the restaurant, sat down, and were trying to order, when all of a sudden the waiter came over and said, "We can't serve this table."

Fielding looked at him: "What do you mean you can't serve this table?"

"It's mixed company."

I knew that the band was mixed, too. They probably didn't know that Mingus, with his light complexion and wavy hair, was black. I didn't want to blow the whistle, but it was weird and we got angry. Red Norvo, a very nice man, came to the table looking like "Don't do that." I guess it was his way of trying to protect the job. It was a good gig, but I don't think I could be that way. I've given up work, man, even when it means I had to lose. I'd probably get up and walk off. Mingus also went along this time. They said, "We can understand you suing and being mad, but why don't you also sue some of the other clubs that are doing it?" We were hurt, and I was surprised at Mingus. I guess they needed the money. So we backed off.

During this period Jerry Fielding was building a big band and he wanted me in it to do some writing with him. I didn't have enough time, and once I heard his writing I felt that he should write alone, because he had a certain style. It was clear to me after hearing his first few arrangements. I would have taken the band in a different direction – not that it would have been better, but I couldn't write in his style. He had everything tightly knit together, more or less all worked out. In my groups I like more freedom to work it out. If the tenor player wants to play an extra chorus, then the arrangement can accommodate. With Jerry's arrangements, you couldn't do that very well. Each of them was calculated to come out perfectly.

It was a very good experience, because Jerry was a hard writer, and since I was working with him on the Groucho Marx show, it was a nice tie-in to something other than just the show. We traveled a lot with the band, but not long distances. We would go to San Diego, Oceanside, places in southern California where there were ballrooms that wanted a good band. We also did some record sessions with Albert Marx, who had Discovery Records, now called Trend Records. He's recorded everybody and has been very helpful. Albert was recording a lot of people in town that no one else would.

Jerry Fielding and HUAC

I saw the House Un-American Activities Committee topple Jerry Fielding from the Groucho Marx show. After I was hired, he began to integrate all of his orchestras. Jerry hired Red Callender on *The Life of Riley* show. He also had a TV jazz band with Red Callender, Gerry Wiggins, and me. The show was sponsored by Aldon Homes, owned by Don Metz, whose daughter, Donna, I later taught flute. Don was a guy that took about $10,000, which was a lot of money, and started building homes in the San Fernando Valley, which at that time was only desert, more or less – just dirt. He went out there and built a lot of tract homes; ten, fifteen of them right away, and sold them. Don made a lot of money and started hanging around the stars and Hollywood. He wanted to publicize his homes with a jazz band fronted by Jerry. We hadn't amalgamated yet, and so Jerry's idea was to have three blacks in the band that could play, all the time thinking, "We've got to get together." He didn't talk that much, but I could see what he was thinking. So he hired Red, Gerry, and me. We were the jazzers in the band and got a lot of solo playing.

It was a great show and the only thing that went wrong was the response to all the exposure we got. The camera was panning us all the time and the show got so much hate mail. This was the early 1950s. The only blacks on TV or in the movies were actors like Stepin Fetchit, Willie Best and Hattie McDaniel. Most of the black women would be maids, seen catching buses, going back and forth, and you could tell by the way they were dressed who they were. The black men were either chauffeurs or doing some kind of garbage and trash collection job. So there we were in suits and being featured. Sometimes I'd walk out to the mike and play. Don just said, "Yeah, a lot of people don't like the show because of what we're doing and who we have in the band, but we're going to go on." We stayed on for a few months, which was great.

Jerry Fielding kept on and it got him into trouble. One night while we were doing the Groucho show, two big guys, about six-foot-four, from the House Un-American Activities Committee served a subpoena on Jerry Feldman (his real name). This could have been 1952 or 1953. When they came in, the show was going on and they kept screaming, "Feldman!"

Ben Barrett, the contractor, said, "The show's going on."

"We want Feldman over there!" They didn't care whether the show was on or not.

Jerry was very nervous; he was trying to conduct, and saw these two guys. Leading up to this, he was getting phone calls every night from someone. It would be two or three in the morning; the phone would ring, and a voice would say, "Feldman, we're going to get you." He wasn't getting much sleep. He knew they were going to do something, but he didn't know what. Finally, when the show had a break, Jerry got off the stand and walked over. They gave him a subpoena. Part of it was because I was in the band. That was a no-no. It was really crucial. I can see it more clearly now. Then I was enjoying just being there, but also wondering, "Why is all this happening?"

Before Jerry appeared at the hearings, he called the band together and said, "Guys, here's the scene: I'm not a communist. They're just after people. If I talk, then I've got to say who I spend time with and they'll have to go through all of this. The lawyers say that the only way is to take the Fifth Amendment. Otherwise they'll keep this thing going. They'll call another fifty people. I'm going to take the Fifth, so you'll understand."

Then one of the guys who had served him the subpoena came over and said, "If you've got $200,000, we'll get you out of this."

Jerry replied, "If I had $200,000 I wouldn't give a shit who you guys were."

You can see how vicious it was, and Jerry was a real straight guy; he was.

For a long time we helped Jerry, because they dropped him from the show. Groucho, Bob Dwan (the director), and John Guedel (the producer) met with Jerry. He said, "Look, this is what's happening and I hope I can keep the show, because it's BS." And they said, "Well, if you don't get a lot of publicity, we'll hang with you." Of course it was front page news: "Groucho Marx's conductor...." All of a sudden they backed away, which was terrible. The guys in the

126

band were making about $130 a week and we chipped in about twenty dollars a week for four or five months, because he was cut off completely. Radio stations wouldn't play his records. I took in one of the records we'd made with his big band, not realizing that they wouldn't play it. The guy saw the record and said, "Get that out of here. We can't play that." The word went around. They also did that to Paul Robeson.

Jerry did very little work for about four or five years. He did some ghost writing, and worked a bit in Las Vegas. He wrote for some shows, but couldn't own up to being the writer, which was tough, because it made him very angry and bitter. He only started writing again when Betty Hutton insisted that Jerry score a picture she was in. "I will not do it unless you get Jerry Fielding." She was very powerful and got her way. He got back in, but was never the same after that. I used to see him and he was the most angry man, because he had been so hurt by all of that.

Jerry Fielding was the kind of fighter that we don't have around very often. He and I got to be good friends, not just because of the music, but we had a lot in common in the battles we fought. As you can see, that period was very frightening for both of us. Many people lost their jobs, because if you did stick your neck out you could lose your gig.

Paul Robeson

During this time Paul Robeson was around doing concerts supported by flute and string quartet. I was introduced to him some years earlier by a woman named Frances Williams, who had her own theater. It was in 1941, just before I went into the navy and when I was playing in Cee Pee Johnson's orchestra. Paul used to come hear the band at the Rhumboogie in Hollywood. I didn't see him again until the late 1940s. By that time the government had begun their campaign to limit his travel and speech rights.

Paul had his story to tell, which was great, and it was a different side than what I had heard before. At Frances' house he'd talk about the attacks on him because of his statements on his trip to Russia: "All I said was that I got treated better there. They treated me like a king. When I get home, they discriminate against my people."

He was a truthful man and I was in awe of him. He was one of the first to speak out in that way and that did a lot for me, to see and hear that. He wasn't afraid. Being around him was a turning period for me; I loved it. At his concerts I was with these string players, playing my heart out, and there was this big man.

Paul spoke at the end of our first concert at the Embassy Auditorium. But it was a period when they didn't want him to speak at all, because too many people would hear him. When he came back a few months later to do it again, the powers-that-be had put up signs: "There will be no public speaking." If he spoke, they could go in during the concert and cart him off to jail. We were all there; we've got our group on stage and the place is packed, complete with government agents in the audience. But he was a giant of a man and you don't stop him much until he dies. He wasn't a rough kind of a guy; he was smart. Paul walked out on stage and saw the signs. Guess what he did? He sang his message! He really did. Imagine that great voice singing, "They can't stop us!" When he finished, he smiled – his shoulders were about as broad as I had ever seen – put his hat on, and walked out.

Many people don't realize the inspiration he gave to a lot of black people who were leaders, who were able to stand up. Because it can be costly if you stand up and say, "I believe in this." He was the kind of person who was true. Without Paul things would have been a lot worse and more difficult to achieve, even what we had achieved with the union. In some way he was responsible for my musical career because his strength and determination were a great inspiration. These kinds of stories are important so that the youth and others can say, "There were many great people, who were doing wonderful things. It didn't just start now."

In his last days he wasn't doing much speaking, but he'd come to LA occasionally. Frances would tell me, "Paul's going to be in town on Sunday. Why don't you come by and bring a girlfriend? It's going to be six or seven of us. We're just going to sit around and have lunch and talk." It was that simple. Paul would tell us what he was doing or might point out, "They're blocking me here," or, "This fight is going on there." He would not be preaching to the point of trying to convince everyone, and we'd all exchange stories. He predicted that we would have a lot of turmoil, and the racial division would go on and on; it would not clear up, and he was right.

Society has changed a lot on that level, but at the same time there's so many aspects that we don't and won't even talk about now. If you ask, "Are things okay today?" I would say, "Well, in certain ways it's better." If we're talking about a thirty-year period of change, think of it as you and I as players, playing for thirty years. We're still in the same book that we were in originally. We might be a couple of pages down the line, but that's not progress to me. If we were doing it properly, we might have been through thirty books by now and everybody would be benefiting on another level. Maybe the change is going to be slow all the time, but we need leaders to help set the pace and to re-emphasize what should be happening. If that means jail, then whatever it takes to say, "We mean this." I don't think that's being done enough.

Once you've seen the struggles

I didn't see myself as that political; I still thought of myself as a musician. But once you see the struggles and you hear all the stories – whether you are white or black – it might mean something a little different. I became aware, after the examples of Paul Robeson and Jerry Fielding, that no matter how great I would get on my instruments, I could be pulled back. Jackie Robinson, as big a star as he was, had a very bad time. Jackie was supposed to be the new hero of the blacks. Then they turned around and said, "He doesn't represent the blacks." So it didn't make me very political, as much as it made me aware of how we can all be used. It made me more aware that if that's what it's all about, then I've got to be good at what I do, and at the same time I have to be helping to change some of those problems. If this continues to exist, it means that we're all still much farther behind than we should be.

So this was a period when I began to look further than just the union fights. I looked at the fights that the American Civil Liberties Union (ACLU) and people like that were doing. It was a great move on my part, because it started me thinking in a different way than just reading the papers and thinking this is the only thing that's going on. During this time I was probably more with the Democrats, but there were times when I was viewing some of the socialist views. Not that I was going along with it, but after meeting a lot of people in the days of the amalgamation, I'd started reading the *People's World* paper, and got some different views. A lot of people would think you were a communist if you were reading it, but I got a view of things that I had never gotten before. It opened up the mind. It's like when you're searching for answers, you need to have more than one sign to understand what's really going on – who's telling the truth, and what are we really talking about. Well, I'm that way about my music, too. There's more than one way to play a song. I think versatility is important.

The ACLU was really struggling when I met them during the early 1950s. I became their band, but I wasn't active, other than musically. Shelly Manne was very active, too, and we'd do many benefits for them. People were being mistreated, or some black in some southern place was accused of rape or whatever, and they'd need money for the case. Whenever I was asked, I'd bring a group. The ACLU had no money to pay anybody, but it wasn't hard. Either I could persuade my group to come along, or I might give them twenty dollars apiece, which was not bad at the time. Many times on a Sunday afternoon, for a fund-raiser, Shelly would call me up and say, "The ACLU called me to do the job with them. Will you?"

"Yeah. What about you?"

"Yeah, let's do it. Let's get a bass player. We can get Monty Budwig, and let's get Al Viola or John Collins, and let's go do it."

It would usually be in somebody's backyard. We just liked the people a lot and the causes they were fighting; not everything, of course, but they were being fair: "We will defend anyone," or, "We will give anyone a chance to say his piece." And I believe in that.

I've been involved through the years, when people needed my services. I told Ramona Ripston, who's the ACLU's executive director, "No fee."

She said, "Well, it's so nice for you all to donate your services, because we don't have any funds."

"It's easy for me to donate what we do for a group like yours, who are working to help so many people. Without you we'd all be in serious trouble. You're keeping the record straight."

That was my feeling. I don't know how political that made me, but I felt that if they're doing that, at least I can bring my saxophone and a rhythm section, and help them win a battle.

12
The Chico Hamilton Quintet

During the mid-fifties I was invited to Lake Tahoe to play with Lena Horne. Chico Hamilton was on drums and Gerry Wiggins was on piano. I worked with them a week and then we all drove back in my car. Chico and I always talked about doing something together, but now he was planning on leaving Lena Horne. Before that Chico had met Fred Katz, a pianist and cellist, who was playing piano with Lena, just before Gerry started. Chico and Fred had also talked about getting a group together. Chico wanted to use Fred on piano and then have him play cello as a soloist between sets, when the band was off the stand. When they had both left Lena, they decided to form a band, and called me.

We had a few rehearsals at my apartment, which went very well. We had Carson Smith on bass, who had worked with Chico in the early Gerry Mulligan band. Then someone told us there was a fine guitar player in town from Cleveland and we found Jim Hall, who was working in a bookstore. When Jim joined us it began to come together, and the Chico Hamilton Quintet was born.

A beer bar in Long Beach

Chico was always out looking for work and promoting the band. The Lighthouse in Hermosa Beach was going strong at that time, always packed. So Chico went to a beer bar called Strollers, just south of Hermosa in Long Beach, and convinced the owner, a guy named Harry Rubin, that he should have live music. The only problem for me was that I was working with Scatman Crothers at the Tailspin Club in Hollywood and I had to give him two weeks notice. So I was

132

going to be about one week late. Chico arranged to get Bob Hard-away to sub for that week and then I joined the band later.

When I finally got there, I couldn't believe the place: nothing but beer drinkers, the six-pack crowd. I told the guys, "I quit my job in Hollywood to join you and this is what you're getting me into?" It wasn't a good spot at all and it took an hour-and-a-half to get to Long Beach from Los Angeles during this pre-freeway era.

The first week I was there, it was kind of quiet, but the band began to play quite well and we really sounded pretty good. We had a three-week contract or something like that. Although it had been kind of quiet, Harry apparently was breaking even. "Well, guys, your three weeks are up, but why don't we just try it a little longer. I do like the band and what you're doing. I'll contact KFOX and see if we can put in radio." He was always a promoting kind of guy. He'd try anything; that's why he always made it. The group was good and whatever publicity he was doing before, it wasn't reaching the people that we needed to reach. So Harry got the radio spot and got Sleepy Stein, who was a good disc jockey, to come in and do a show right from Strollers. That week we were on the radio half-an-hour on Monday, Wednesday and Friday nights.

We couldn't believe the next weekend. People were standing around the corner to get in the club. Our music was different and it just drew them. People would come in and say, "We were on our way to San Diego and we just had to find out where this place was with this kind of music." With most music you could predict what was going to happen, but ours was different. We didn't know what we were doing half the time, but we were having fun and the group kept getting better and growing.

At this point Fred was playing cello, not piano, all the time and that came about by accident. At first, he'd play solo cello during the intermissions, and Fred's the kind of guy who would play a long time. He'd play half-an-hour, if you let him. Fred's very energetic. But we only needed fifteen minutes. The bandstand was so small and the piano was in the back. After fifteen minutes or so we'd just get on the stand while Fred was playing cello, deep in meditation, and then all of a sudden he'd open his eyes and we'd all be there. Chico was ready to do something with his sticks and would start a number, usually improvised. Fred would stay where he was, because he couldn't get back to the piano unless we got off and let him walk through. So he'd continue playing on the cello, trying to find some of the lines that he'd been playing on the piano. All of us at the same time began to realize that we were going to get him away from the piano, because as he played the lines on cello, the group sounded completely different.

This gave Jim Hall more freedom to play his way. Jim is a very sensitive player. When Fred was playing piano, Jim would not play as much guitar. Fred's very aggressive and he fills in everything. Jim was just saying, "Well, if you're playing that much, I'll stay out of your way." But we knew what Jim could do. Occasionally Chico used to call "concerts in miniature," where we might do something with just guitar, bass and me, or a smaller combination. Now, without the piano and Fred on cello, suddenly we could hear the guitar, and the overall group sound was much cleaner. We loved that, though without saying it. We just kept writing things that kept Fred on the cello and that's how it started. With Jim playing the chords, we had more freedom. We didn't need two sets of chords going, especially since both guys didn't play chords at all alike. They were in two different worlds. Fred's a very classical type of guy in his approach to just about everything. Jim's got the classical background, but he's into jazz; he thinks that way and he plays that way. And he plays very sparse-like. He knows just what to do and when; he has sensitivity. He's listening to you and accompanying you in the best way. When that sound came together, we knew where we were going and we started to write in that same way.

The Chico Hamilton Quintet did what could be considered chamber jazz, and although we all wrote, we did more improvisation. We didn't even need music, although we did have a lot of things written down. Fred Katz liked to write everything out. Jim Hall sometimes would write pieces out. But 50 percent of the time we'd just play, improvise, not even discussing what we would play. Somebody would start a line and the line would continue with answers, fugue statements, recapitulations, and those kinds of things. The ideas would move around and come back at you like an echo. It might have begun with just a look, and before we knew it, all our minds would be locked into one. We'd frequently get requests for certain pieces, but couldn't play them again for any amount of money. They were one-time-only pieces that depended on what our experiences had been to that point and what we felt at that moment. Even pieces that were written would continually change, because of the way we approached the solos. A day or a week or two later, we might have found a different way to approach a tune. Although the listener would hear the same melody, the piece would change.

There was great sensitivity in each musician. Chico, the leader, was very unusual with his rhythms and was always sensitive to what the group was doing. Whenever we were improvising, he seemed to find the right balance. If I was playing flute, clarinet, or tenor, he knew the right approach with his instrument. We were that close; we phrased and lived together; knew each other's habits, just like family life. It really paid off, because we began to extract our style from improvisation and then most of our writing was centered around that. Everyone had music; everyone was writing. Two or three times a week, in the afternoon, we'd rehearse at the club to get this new music together. We'd run over three or four numbers for the night; we all had time to do it and liked doing it. Then we'd go have dinner and hit the bandstand.

"Blue Sands"

With the crowds we started attracting at Strollers, we knew we had to record. We invited some of the record companies, who were around at the time: Contemporary, Pacific Jazz, Challenge Records, Sy Warniker's Liberty Records. The big companies came out, but a lot of them didn't know what our music was, because it was different and they weren't sure if they wanted to record it. "Gosh, it's jazz, but it's so different." The only guy that really took a bite was Dick Bock from World Pacific Records. He brought his equipment down to

Strollers and recorded for about three days at the club. On the first Chico Hamilton Quintet album there were five live tracks from Strollers. We then went into the studio and did five more, so we'd have a balance with the live material. Between the live tapings and the studio recordings, we were able to get a good presentation of the group.

"Blue Sands," one of my compositions, was on that first album. I knew it was a very unusual piece the first time I played it. It was written just for my flute exercises. When I first began to play flute, I wanted to build up my embouchure, and I felt that high notes and wide intervals would help. So in the beginning it wasn't a piece, but a flute exercise with wide intervals. I had played it one night during a gig at the California Club on Santa Barbara Avenue, which is now Martin Luther King, Jr. Boulevard. The club had been opened by Gene Norman and its first band was the newly formed Max Roach and Clifford Brown group. That was around 1953. In 1954 I played there with a quartet on the weekends, and the place was packed. I had Ernie Freeman on piano, Larry Bunker on drums, and Buddy Woodson on bass. The show also had a singer and a dancer. We would open the show with a fast band number each night and each time it was very noisy. The people were whooping it up with the drinks on the table and a lot of noise. Nobody seemed to care. So one Friday night I thought, "Tomorrow night I'll just play that little flute line to see if they're really listening."

The next night I told the guys to play that line. Since the rhythm parts are very simple, I just told them on the bandstand what to play. Ernie Freeman always had great ears. The bass has a counter line and the drummer plays mallets. "Once you hear the melody, just go for yourself. Open up. Let's play." We got into it. I took the flute and played the line, and it took about fifteen seconds before the house got so quiet I couldn't believe it. People stopped talking and started looking, as if to say, "What's going on?" They hadn't heard this kind of approach. Each night we'd been doing a flag waver, just romping on tenor and drum solos. They just talked through that. This time they didn't talk through it. They liked the piece a lot, and applauded. "What do we have here?" I thought.

136

When I got together with Chico and we were looking for new material, I pulled out "Blue Sands" and the same thing happened. We got to the point where it would last for at least twelve minutes. We could not stop it; it would always go longer, because once you got in and started telling your story, you couldn't back away. It became one of our most requested tunes. "Blue Sands" had such a mood and the audience would just sit there. We wouldn't know what they were thinking. It seemed to have a hypnotic kind of control over the public, but it also seemed that each one would reminisce in their own way. You could see it. Whatever it meant to you, whatever it meant to me, it always made people kind of quiet. We never played it twice in the same evening. It just wasn't that kind of tune. We might play other things twice, even though we didn't like to, but we had to put too much into "Blue Sands" to repeat it. That's the kind of piece it was.

When the band reunited briefly some thirty years later, we played "Blue Sands" in Verona, Italy, in 1989, and it was amazing how we sounded. Guitarist John Pisano really got into it. I looked at him, and the music seemed to jump out and grab him. The mood got him and he just kept playing, kept building; it was great. "Take as long as you want." That's the way you feel. It's a feeling you get with the counter-bass part, the drum mallets, and the mood of that modal scale. When it all comes together, it really works for us.

The liner notes on our first album came about in a funny way. Dick Bock, the producer, invited us to dinner at his home after we'd finished the album. Dick had this big table with a nice flowerpot in the middle. He asked us what we felt and what we were trying to do with the band.

"By the way, what were you thinking about when you played that?"

I'd say, "Well, we were just trying to do what we thought was best. Some people will probably say I'm playing differently now, but my feeling is that if you're a sensitive player you're playing for what group you're in. There's no reason for me to sound like I'm in another band. If I hear cello and guitar, I'm playing to fit that sound."

After we finished dinner and the evening was winding down, Dick laughed a little and said, "Well, we've got our notes." Somehow he had placed a microphone, without us knowing, in the large flowerpot on the table and kept it on during our conversation. The liner notes are a little different, but Dick was able to get nice quotes from everybody.

On the road

That was the beginning of the group and we took off with our first album, which sold a lot. We got all kinds of offers to go to New York, Chicago, and Europe. We went to the Newport Jazz Festival in 1956. We played on Sunday evening and were the next to last group, which was Duke Ellington's orchestra. Everybody there was exhausted after three or four days of jazz. No one sleeps very much when you hang out and party all night. Clarinetist Tony Scott had all-night jam sessions. It was just a madhouse for three or four days.

Our band got on at nine o'clock that Sunday night. The only problem was that by the time we went on stage, everyone was either falling asleep or very tired. We played most of our best material – "A Nice Day," "Funny Valentine" – and got nice applause, but nothing earthshaking like we thought we should get, like we were getting around the country before Newport. We still hadn't reached them, and it's hard to get off the stand without trying to make them really scream, especially with Ellington coming up.

Toward the end of our set Chico looked at me. We had about ten minutes before we were through. "Well, do you think we should play 'Blue Sands'?" We weren't sure. It might put them further to sleep. At this point we thought that maybe we needed something to wake the audience up. But I said, "We've played everything else. We'd better try it."

The Quintet got into it and played and played and played. It easily took the rest of the set. With "Blue Sands" you have to keep playing until you finish your mood, and only then can you taper off, end your solo. As we played and then started tapering off, I looked out at about six, seven thousand people. You could see the heads and the dark silhouettes. They weren't moving; it looked like they were frozen. No one said anything. Smoke had been rising up from cigarettes, but even that seemed to have stopped. The piece was that hypnotic. I thought, "This may have been a mistake. Let's get out of here; we've blown it." But we just kept playing; we couldn't give up. How do you know if you're winning or losing? We finally ended the piece with a triple piano, the softest we'd ever done. Chico was on mallets and I was trilling on the flute, walking away from the mike. For about ten seconds we just stood there with our hearts pounding. No one moved, no applause, nothing. Then, suddenly, the crowd leapt up, out of the trance. They screamed and shouted, and we'd never heard anything quite like that. It was wild, because that was the biggest ovation that anyone had received up to this point in the Festival. With this group there was just no way to know what was going to happen.

As we came off the bandstand, we were very happy; we were a hit. We had waited four hours to go on and it felt great. As I exited, carrying all my horns, I walked right into Duke Ellington. He was smiling, Mr. Personality, and said, "Wow! You all made it hot for me, didn't you?" I almost wanted to apologize, to tell him that we didn't mean to! But Duke and his band were fired up. He loved it that way; he loved a challenge. Like a great tennis player or a fighter, he's better if he's got someone encouraging him to use his best works. And that's what happened. We left the stage hot and Duke went out, waving his arms, and his band really got into it. They did "Diminuendo and Crescendo in Blue," and Paul Gonsalves took that great solo.

It was a fabulous period for us. We had a new, exciting group and all of us were very enthusiastic. We all wrote and we had plenty of music. We loved to rehearse and were very successful. We had a good combination of people and part of the magic was that we lived like a family for a while. There was a togetherness. Nowadays it's a little harder to get that. People are busy and running, but the togetherness is what makes the difference with groups. There's a lot of communication that lets you know each other, when the instant kind of thing has to happen. You instantly come up with a crescendo and then back out of the way, and it may not even be marked. You'd say, "I knew you were going to do that." There's a kinship there.

I was with Chico's group for a year and a half. I eventually left because I couldn't pass up the opportunities I had back in Los Angeles. I had been on the Groucho Marx show for a few years, and for a half-an-hour show I made as much as I would out on the road for a week's work. Traveling with Chico there were a lot of one-nighters. We would make $250, $300 a week at that time, but we worked hard for it; always changing hotels and constant traveling in the cars. The studios meant short hours and a lot of money, every week, and I knew that it would lead to other things. It led to a lot of studio work with some of the finest musicians in the world, and learning how to be a first-class studio player.

It was the right move, because when you're out on the road all the time you're constantly trying to prove that you've got a good group and the group's going to make a lot of money one day. But that's the hard way of doing it. I think I made myself more valuable by not doing too much of it, doing enough so they knew who I was, and going to Europe and Japan later on and doing records. Chico wasn't a studio player. He always wanted to be a leader, and is. He's out there right now. But I'd rather be a leader three or four weeks, come home, then maybe go back, because one-nighters are very hard. And you've got to allow yourself time to write and to practice. When you're out on the road – where you work nine-to-one, go and eat breakfast, get home at three, and up the next morning at eight because you have to be traveling that day – it's very hard; very tough on the individual, physically and mentally. You stay tired. So I was able to make the adjustment and move to what I thought was a better way.

13
The studio scene

Back home, I was writing and studying. I had a family and I needed the money. The Groucho Marx show was very steady financially and I had plenty of time off to keep studying flute, saxophone, and clarinet – three or four days off – an ideal situation. I felt I should devote myself to getting better on my instruments and rehearsing with many groups, learning to play and read better. I thought, "If I can continue like this, I can make it." I had the best of everything: a nice car and an apartment, and my family was being cared for after I broke up with Louise. Without the Groucho job it would have been a scuffle during that period.

Living in two worlds

To make it in the studios you need the practice time, because it is tough. You must play most charts at first sight, so you have to become like a fighter always in top shape. When I would go out and play gigs, I would always try to get in a couple of hours before I left the house. It's on your mind all the time. You don't ever want to be caught in a situation where they might pass out a piece and you can't handle it. It's not only embarrassing, but you could lose a lot of work. If they needed a change of vibrato, for example, I could just do it. The lead alto player on the Groucho Marx show, Hynie Gunkler, kept saying, "Gosh, you're really one of the guys who knows how to blend in with us."

I also had an advantage with the flute. It began to get popular around 1950, 1951, 1952. Before then most saxophone players just played clarinets and saxophones. When it became in demand for

141

saxophone players to have clarinet and flute also, I was ready. I had been playing for ten years or so, and had played flute during the Stars of Swing period. That gave me some experience playing before an audience, and some confidence on the instrument as well. By the time the red light went on in the studio, I wasn't as frightened as somebody who'd just practiced at home.

The studios also demand other, unusual instruments, such as alto and bass clarinets. I didn't get into the contrabass clarinet too much. I do have one, because J.J. Johnson, the fine trombone player and writer, was doing a series, and kept saying, "Do you play contrabass clarinet? I'm going to need one on this show. If you had one, I could let you do most of the calls." I figured, "What the heck?" So I bought one. I made the cost of the instrument back after three or four sessions. I also played a lot of piccolo, alto flute, and bass flute. I don't have a bass sax, but I have a baritone sax. At one period I was willing to play them all. Now I'm not so much into bass clarinet and baritone sax, unless it's for my own recordings. It means more to me now to do it only on my own music, or something else that I want to be a part of. There comes a time when you want to pick and choose what you do.

I did studio work not because I thought it was the greatest, but because I was challenged by it. I worked hard not to play just my own music, but to be able to get on in the studio. At the same time, I did have a pretty good jazz quintet, and took many weekend jobs. I devoted a lot of time to making sure our band was better than most of the others. At the club jobs that were happening, if you knew enough tunes you could work. But I just didn't see the future in clubs as much as I did in studio work, because I'd met a lot of guys who did studio work and they had homes and investments. Very few musicians working the clubs had that; they were worrying about the rent.

It was like living in two worlds. There were the so-called jazz guys, who only did the clubs on a Friday or Saturday night, or a jam session, and they'd be trying to borrow a couple of bucks from you. Then I'd meet this other group of people – studio players – and they were talking about building and selling homes. Right away you'd get a feeling: "Now, this is more inviting. I could stay in LA and wouldn't have to go out on the road." There are times when you have to take some jobs that are more based on need, so you won't play and starve. Who are the true artists?

That's the picture of the 1950s, how it just began to grow. There was a lot of work. There was writing. We did all kinds of shows. I worked quite a bit with Bill Green and he got married during this time. It might have been 1957, 1958. I was so busy then that it all runs together. When Bill got married, his idea was to gather all his musician friends. He called Ben Webster, Bumps Myers, Sig Galloway, who was also a tenor player, and Clyde Dunn, one of Bill's students. After the ceremony Bill had a long table set up with some instruments laid out: a tenor, alto, and soprano saxophones. Everything was in order, but he didn't get a rhythm section. Bill wasn't thinking jam session, but he did want to hear everyone play. The rest of us didn't quite know what was going on. "Is this a Selmer show or what?"

Ben Webster, always a character, said, "What are you doing, Bill? Showing off your horns?"

"Well, I think everybody should play a little something. I think we all should play a little tune."

We all agreed, knowing that this was really his wish; just something from all his favorite people. So Galloway, who was an interesting player, not very studied, but always with a blues feeling, probably honked a little, wild blues. He wasn't shy, so he picked up one of the horns first, and did his thing. Three or four more guys played. Then Bill gave a horn to Bumps Myers, who was a good player and used to work with Benny Carter. Bumps always loved his little taste and drank a lot, but he was a very nice guy with a big smile. Bumps went into something pretty, but definitely just the way Ben would play, one of those pretty things down in the low end of the tenor. Bumps thought it would be a compliment, but Ben didn't like it and he looked angry. He didn't say much, but you could see him frowning. Then I played and, finally, everyone except Ben.

Very politely, Bill said, "Ben, it's your turn."

"Man, I'm not going to play. This man's already played me!"

Bill kept at him, "Man, you know, my wedding. . . ."

143

Finally, Ben agreed to play something. He got the horn, put it in his mouth, and ... nothing, just a burst of air came out of that horn. "What the. . . .," and he tried it again. Still just air.

Then Bill leaned over and said, "Ben, take in a little more mouthpiece."

We screamed, everyone together, because you don't tell Ben Webster anything!

He looked at Bill and said, "Bill, you tell that to your students!"

Everybody just hollered again. Ben didn't appreciate that at all. Bill could get away with it, because they liked each other so much, but, even then, that was dangerous. Ben was noted for hitting people for less. That was a classic, very funny day. Ten, fifteen years later, guys would still lean over to Bill and say, "Bill, take in a little more mouthpiece." And Bill would reply, "Be nice, now. Be nice."

Frank Sinatra

This was a very busy time for me. For a period of two or three years in the 1950s everything was happening and overlapping. Morning, noon and night there was activity, and not just working, but also meeting people, rehearsing, writing, studying, practicing. I was studying with three teachers at the same time, and I was working on the Groucho Marx show, *You Bet Your Life*.

I met Nelson Riddle, who was a big writer at the time and with whom I'd work a great deal, especially on Sinatra dates. But the first record I did with him was a date for Billy Eckstine. Nelson came into the Crescendo Club, where we were working with Jerry Fielding, walked over to me and said, "We've got a record date on Thursday. It's with Billy Eckstine, and I would like you to play flute and saxophone." I was impressed, of course, because I knew who Nelson was. I don't think I knew what he looked like, but here was someone who was like a regular guy, who walked up and said, "Hey, I'm Nelson Riddle."

"What?"

Naturally, I accepted the call, but when I got to the date – and I'll never forget this – he wasn't conducting. Nelson was signed with another record company, Capitol Records, at the time, but had written the arrangements and was standing in the back room, helping whoever was conducting. He probably had to do that to protect his contract. And whoever was conducting was there because of Nelson. But I remember the date very well. I got to play his music and he noticed a flute solo of mine. It was an introduction to Nelson Riddle in a great way, and I began to work with him quite a bit after that.

Nelson deserves a lot of credit, musically and otherwise. Musically, because he had something very special in accompanying singers like Sinatra, Rosemary Clooney, and Nat King Cole. He had a knack for making arrangements that fit the personalities. In the band we could see what a difference it would make. He didn't even have great tempos, but he was a genius for backing singers. In another area, Nelson hired people based only on their ability. Early on he hired Sweets Edison, Plas Johnson, Bill Green, and me. His only standard was whether or not they could play. He was a very fair man and his success was great and deserved. It was a shame that we lost him.

In the fifties we were doing a lot of Sinatra and Nat King Cole albums. I was the featured tenor soloist with the band. Usually I would get a solo or something interesting to play. The first time I recorded with Sinatra, we were doing a piece called "Tell Her You Love Her." Nelson was there, and also the writer of the tune, but I can't think of his name. We did a take and finally another one. Sinatra was uncanny in the way he would just know if it was a good take or not. Sometimes he didn't have to listen to the playback; he just knew it. There were times when he would say, "That's it!" and run out of the studio. It's like a good kicker in football; he doesn't even have to look, just runs off the field. That's the way he was and it did usually feel right. There might be a bad note here and there, but that wouldn't bother him. That was part of his charm and part of his talent. And he was a very talented man, and had great musical taste. I'm not sure how much music he knew, but he did know how to get the most out of arrangements. For

145

example, he would know to use two cellos instead of three in a passage to get a certain sound.

After we finished "Tell Her You Love Her," Frank listened. The orchestra was talking a little bit and he said, "Quiet!" When he said "Quiet," he meant it, and everyone was very quiet. I had an eight-bar tenor solo and everyone just listened. I listened, too, and I thought the solo was okay. At the end of the tenor solo, Frank just laughed. He didn't say "Hey, I liked that," or anything. He was a very unusual guy and I guess that meant he liked it.

A lot of times you don't know what people really think of you, and this was a chance to figure it out. Sinatra was a very unusual man; he didn't like everybody, and was very opinionated. Sometimes he'd arrive for a record date, look up, and say, "Hi, Bud," out of thirty people. Some guys would ask, "How do you rate?" I didn't think I had done anything. He was that kind of guy. There was once an article in the European *Melody Maker* magazine, where Frank talked about six jazz players he liked. My name was in there. So it was just one of those wild things.

Frank liked to have great parties. He had one at his house in Beverly Hills, and had me get a group. I guess we were friends, if you can call it that, because he'd never call me. The only time I'd ever see him would be on a recording date or something like that. At this party he had about ten people there: Robert Mitchum and eight or nine people who were big stars, and a couple of other friends who were with their lady friends. We didn't have to play very much, because they had a sit-down dinner and we'd watch TV or talk most of the time. We played a little in the beginning. While they had dinner, Frank had one of my albums, *Calm, Cool, Collette*, playing through that whole time. Here was a guy telling you something without showing you.

Frank had a temper of course. When things didn't go his way, it would come out. Once he was supposed to go to Australia and, apparently, someone bumped one of the musicians who was supposed to have a sleeping berth in one of the big planes. Sinatra canceled the whole tour. "If you bump one of us from this flight, then we won't go." After a few weeks Frank had a change of heart and wanted to make up the lost money for the promoters. So Sinatra and Nelson Riddle's band, without Nelson, did a tour in the States. Anytime Frank wanted to tour, it was going to be successful, especially at that time. We did many auditoriums and concert halls, two cities a day when the cities were close. We could do an afternoon show from two o'clock to four, get on the plane, and be in another city and state that evening to play again. And the band played very well each time.

In those days Frank was a drinker – Jack Daniels straight. One day during this tour Sinatra came on the plane and his eyes were red and he had an ice pack, almost like a cap, that fit on his head. He was out of it, and we knew that no one in the band should talk to him. Frank kept talking about his daughter, Nancy, who just had her nineteenth birthday, and that was bothering him. He couldn't believe that she was that old. He had someone deliver her a brand-new Thunderbird, a pink one, wrapped in cellophane.

This time Frank also showed his feeling for me. He got on the plane carrying a portable record player that played 45s. I was sitting next to Joe Comfort, who was the bass player. Frank put it in back of my headrest, picked out a record and cranked up the volume. It was a tune of mine called "Monorail." I said, "Hey, where did you get that?"

And he said, "I know what you're doing!" and walked away.

Very strange. Frank knew me, but had never talked to me. He seemed shy, but not really; just didn't talk. He never said to me, "I heard your band." But somehow he found a record of mine that was not easy to find, and played it a lot.

I went to the John F. Kennedy presidential inauguration in 1961 with Frank and had some of the worst experiences during that little three- or four-day gig. The meat of this story was being discriminated against in Arlington, Virginia. There was almost a riot there because of me. The plane landed in Washington, DC, and we took buses to Arlington. Everyone in the band wanted to go to this place to eat breakfast. I was unpacking. Joe Comfort was my roommate and he decided not to go eat. I said I'd go. This area felt like the deep South; we were the only two black guys in the band, and Joe was very light-skinned. Our girl singer, Sue Raney, was also with the band on this trip. She was about twenty years old, blonde, and a beautiful young lady. As I was heading down the road, Sue yelled, "Buddy! Wait for me!"

This frightening feeling came over me, because I knew that many people were not going to like this.

There was a young black guy doing windows outside the restaurant, strictly southern-looking with a hat on, about nineteen years old. He looked at Sue and me walking in as if to say, "Please don't do that; you're not going to make it." Some of the other musicians were already in the restaurant, about five or six of them at a big table. Sue and I went in, sat down, and right away I heard scurrying and phones being dialed. I was thinking about what to order, but I could hear that trouble was brewing. A waiter came over, stood right behind me, and said, "We can't serve this table."

Someone else asked, "What do you mean? We want our eggs."

Nobody was catching it, except Dick Noel, our trombone player.

"Buddy, let's get out of here quick!"

But I couldn't move; I couldn't react and I'm aware of all this happening around me. It was like a bad dream.

"Buddy, let's go. Come on, right now!"

Then I got up and started walking out with Dick. The rest of the guys said, "Where are you guys going?" No one else had caught it yet. Dick had been on the road with Tommy Dorsey when jazz trumpeter Charlie Shavers was in that band. Right away Dick realized what could happen.

We got out to the road just as the cops arrived, not a minute to spare. They didn't come after us. The other musicians came out to see what was going on. It had been raining and there were mud puddles around. About six or eight cops on motorcycles splashed water on the other musicians, anything to make them feel terrible. Who knows what they would have done if I hadn't left? If Dick hadn't called me, I might have been sitting there. When we got back to the motel, we called Sinatra and he was pretty mad about all of this. He put us in a big hotel in Washington, DC, and laid down the law:

"Nothing better happen. These guys get first-rate treatment."

Hollywood and Calvin Jackson

Long before I met Calvin Jackson, I'd heard that he had been hired by MGM – the first black composer and musician to work there full-time. This was about 1940 or 1941, just before I went into the service. He was under Georgie Stoll, who was the head of the music department. André Previn came in later and was under Calvin. So Calvin was second in line. He was about twenty, twenty-one years old at the time and Previn was seventeen or eighteen.

At MGM there was always a lot of piano work, beautiful piano playing in the movies, and Calvin improvised a lot of that. There might be a big scene and he would play piano for three, four, five minutes, just lovely stuff. They'd turn the tape on, let it run, and he'd capture the mood. He also did a lot of scoring on many pictures. I don't even remember what the names are now, but there were many times when Georgie Stoll would turn all the writing over to him.

Calvin was such an excellent pianist. Shortly after he came to Los Angeles, he went to Alex Lovejoy's, an upstairs, after-hours place at Vernon and Central Avenue, where they were having a jam session that night, and Art Tatum was there. Whenever Art showed, a lot of players would try to get in and play with him. Calvin wanted to play for Tatum, to show him how well he could play. He was told, "Well, Tatum hasn't played yet, but if you want to play, go ahead." So Calvin played and he could really get around on the piano, play classical, jazz, anything. Tatum had this thing of listening to all the piano players who were there before he played, always sipping his beer and just looking a little out of one eye. By the time Calvin finished playing, Tatum had worked his way over to the piano. After playing all the piano that anyone could play, Art ended with "Little Man, You've Had a Busy Day." That was his way of telling Calvin and everyone, "You want to play the piano? This is how."

The racial situation at MGM was pretty rough and it was not easy for Calvin. He didn't get much credit for his writing and there were a lot of rules that applied to him, but didn't apply to others doing the same work. He would drive his white convertible through the main gates with his white girlfriend or sometimes with a few starlets, and

149

would get reprimanded for it. He was also playing a lot of clubs and had many friends dropping by to hear him. Every once in a while he'd say, "Hey, come to the session with me." They'd drive in and he'd be told, "You can't do this. You're only the composer." But he realized what was happening.

One thing led to another and MGM and Calvin began to fall out more and more. There might have been things that Calvin was doing, because he was a personality. He could be late at times and was hanging out and doing clubs, but musically he was right on target. He was a great writer, a great talent, and knew what he was doing. Finally, he left and moved to Toronto, Canada. This could have been the mid to late 1940s. He felt he'd be treated more fairly there and did get great treatment there that he never got here. He had been married before, but then married an English lady and had two or three kids. They moved to Canada, figuring that they would not run into the problems they had here as a racially mixed couple. I'm not sure how long that marriage lasted, but Calvin was married again to another woman, Hernesha, when he died in San Diego in 1985.

Oscar Peterson was also from that same area of Canada and probably heard Calvin play a lot. Calvin was the kind of guy you should hear. When somebody is playing that much piano, you have to notice. I'm sure Oscar heard him as a young man, because Calvin could influence you on any instrument.

Calvin was still in Toronto in 1956, when we went there with the Chico Hamilton Quintet. When we arrived, the word was out: "Hey, have you heard Calvin Jackson? He's one of the biggest guys in town." He played a tape for us of a performance he gave at the Town Hall in Toronto. It was a Calvin Jackson night and Calvin did almost everything that's possible for one person to do. He had written a ballet and he conducted it using the symphony orchestra. He played a major piano work – of course from memory – and then had his own jazz group on at the end of the evening with vibe player Peter Appleyard. All this in one night. From eight to about eleven-thirty, except for the intermission, Calvin was on stage doing something different. We couldn't get over this tape. It was just unbelievable.

He was a talent; he was a hard worker, but never seemed to quite make it, even though he made money. When we'd walk down the street in Toronto, people would run over to get his autograph. It was great to see. He was a real star there, but he kept wondering, "What's happening in Hollywood?" I encouraged him to come back, told him that things were changing. I was doing the Groucho Marx show; Benny Carter was working and writing a lot for movies, as were a number of black composers and leaders; Quincy Jones was getting very busy. So Calvin said he'd think about it.

He did return to Los Angeles about one year later, in the mid-fifties, and I tried to help him get work, as much as I could. He played with my quartet. In fact, we did a record for Les Koenig's Contemporary Records, *Nice Day with Buddy Collette*, which was my second album with Les. Calvin did some big projects, like *Rhapsody in Blue Revisited*. That was when he used Eric Dolphy. Calvin just loved Eric's playing, as I mentioned before. He had received a grant to score the Gershwin piece; he got the okay from the Gershwin estate and we made the recording for Capitol Records. It was a great record. It was mainly written; nobody had any real wild solos. He just stayed with the main themes.

Yet Calvin was unhappy while he was in Los Angeles. He had a steady gig at Frascatti's Restaurant on Sunset Boulevard, basically a piano bar setting. He dressed in his tux, played all this classical music and jazz, but he was never the hit that you thought a great piano player should be. He didn't sing, and many of his tempos were fast, so he could show you how well he played the piano. But most people in those bars were drinking and didn't know who this guy was, and would ask him to play pieces that he didn't like. Calvin tried to be very congenial, but I'm pretty sure it bothered him. It was noisy, and he was on a high level of musicianship. He felt he was in a concert hall, even though there might be just Calvin and a bass player. That would go on for a while, then he'd get bothered and quit. And he was having trouble with his family. His kids were growing up, and he and his wife began to have problems.

His manager, Al Sapproff, tried to book him on studio jobs in Hollywood. They finally did get a picture for Calvin, but only because he and Calvin were going to all these different meetings of the American Civil Liberties Union (ACLU), Congress of Racial Equality (CORE), and Career-Oriented Preparation for Employment (COPE), groups who were trying to get better employment for blacks and minorities. Calvin wouldn't say much, but Al would get up and say something like, "I have probably one of the finest composers, black or white, with me tonight, and we can't even get a job for him." They had sent in tapes to all of the studios and had tried everything.

I would loan him a little money at times, because he had two daughters and he was a very proud guy. There were other problems. Even when he was a leader, he'd be late. A couple of times I got him a recording job with Benny Carter, who knew Calvin was in town, at Universal Pictures. The job would start at 9 a.m., and Calvin would come in at nine-thirty. That doesn't work in studio playing. He was like a star, the way he'd come in: "Hey, guys. How are you doing?" Benny would be looking at him, saying, "It's been half-an-hour." So Calvin got hurt on that, because they don't want anyone coming in late and they don't care how great you are. If they say nine o'clock, that's what they mean.

Even with his past it was difficult coming back. I think he figured, "Gosh, I'm good, so after a couple of months I should have a position." Forget it. I know that didn't happen for Benny Carter. When you need the work, it never comes. When Benny, Quincy, and Oliver Nelson arrived in town, the call had come to them. They didn't come in seeking work; they already had positions. It didn't mean that they had more talent, but when they came here, they were able to dictate some of their own terms and what they would like to have. These are the people that are sought after. Calvin came in and it was like, "I've got my family here and I need the work." They don't respond to that. If you need the work, you may not get it. Calvin tried everything for a couple of years and couldn't get a thing.

Finally, a job did happen. It was a film with Jim Brown, the football player – *Tic-Tac-Toe*. Calvin did the score. He was able to dictate what size orchestra he had, and he got good money, although probably not as much as a more established writer, but I'm sure he was thinking that this was going to open a lot of doors for him. When I saw and heard the score that he had written, I got a sinking feeling.

Calvin was still writing in the forties big band style. He had the saxes playing soli's and the screaming trumpets. The musicians began to embrace him and say, "Man, this music is coming back! This is it!" I kept getting a feeling: "Wait a minute. These producers are not going to go for this." Maybe you can get away with it on the titles, but not down in the picture with the dusty roads and that type of thing. We got through the score and Calvin was happy, on top of the world. He felt he could still write; he had his favorite people on the date and everyone went away happy.

Four or five months later, the picture hit the streets and I went to see it. After the opening credits his music was all gone. They had rerecorded a small group of six or seven musicians with a flute, guitar, and drums, all very basic stuff, little folk themes and material like that. When Calvin heard what had happened, it just about killed him; he wanted to leave town.

Calvin and his wife moved down to San Diego, to La Jolla. I used to see him every now and then, when I'd go down there. He'd come out and sit in with me, and many times he'd say, "Things any better in LA? Hollywood?"

"Well, basically the same."

And he'd say, "I'm glad I'm here," or something like that.

San Diego was better for him, just like Toronto was. He achieved a little more of what he wanted, but he was still playing the older material. If he was around today, he'd still be playing "Four Brothers." I don't think I've played "Four Brothers" in thirty or forty years. I probably wouldn't call it, because it's just the wrong tempo; it's the wrong everything for now. It was good for that period, the way the people were dancing and the way they were listening to the big bands.

Calvin was a fighter and never gave up. He felt that one day he would get to record his special material, which he had written out, all of his original music for thirty-five pieces, for twenty-eight pieces. He would call me from San Diego: "Buddy, could you tell me what it would be per man per week, if we did a concert or we go on the road? Can you give me a price?" I knew he was just bouncing ideas off me, trying to keep his dream alive. But his wife was getting pretty discouraged and she was working a day job, hoping that their dream was going to happen. They were living in an apartment in La Jolla. It was so small and close to the other apartments that their wall was right next to somebody else's bathroom, and he couldn't play the piano there. So he didn't practice at home. He'd say, "We'll have to move to a bigger apartment." His wife was doing a great job without much money coming in, but she looked worn out and had been through this many times. Everytime someone visited, Calvin would go through his whole routine, getting very excited about his band and making plans: "We're going to take our thirty-two piece orchestra around the world." A lot of dream talk.

Once in the mid-eighties, in La Jolla, I got a job at the Blue Parrot, and called to offer Calvin the piano chair. I could pay him $250 a night for the weekend, Friday through Sunday. He said, "I don't want to work, because I'm trying to keep my image as a conductor. I will only work if it's my own music. I'll come and sit in, but I'd rather not work and let them see that I can be hired." He came and sat in, played for over an hour-and-a-half the first night, and then came back the next night. Calvin wound up playing at least half of both nights and didn't make any money. He was that proud.

Finally, his wife started getting sick and he had to find some work. He decided to take a job. It was around Thanksgiving and he worked that Tuesday and Wednesday. The next day, he and his wife were returning home from a Thanksgiving dinner. They'd had a great time – good food and a lot of fun. Calvin and Hernesha were both in a great frame of mind. As they were driving, he began to feel pains and had a heart attack. He died in the car, or shortly after that. He never made it to his Friday night job.

This is a story about a guy who was extremely talented and never quite made it to the heights he should or could have. Maybe a lot of it was his own doing. Calvin had made it on an earlier style of music. He helped establish that style and he knew it was good. He walked away and left town because of other problems. When he came back, he thought he could pick up where he left off, but the game had changed by then. He would ask me, "Are they still playing that terrible music in Hollywood? I hope it changes so we can get back to the real thing."

Musically, Calvin was straight; his music was there. He was not BSing. But you've got to do what the people want in many cases. I don't mean you always have to play down to the lowest level, but you have to be somewhere in the current trends. He just didn't understand that no one is going to give him his own TV show, *The Calvin Jackson Hour*, or something like that. That's what he was trying to convince people could happen, but it didn't happen. He was constantly imagining jobs that would cost money. "If we could get about two million here, we could really pull this off." And I'm thinking, "Boy, how do you think that way?" I could never do it.

I think part of Calvin's difficulties stemmed from his coming in as a big, important guy at the early age of nineteen or twenty. He got a taste of it. I wonder if that's the way to do it. When you come in with it that early, and if later you don't have it, all you know is what it should be. You haven't come up with some hard knocks, and you've had steaks and all the best food in the world, and all of a sudden it goes away. Well, you've got trouble. The other way you're adjusting to life. That leads to a different kind of appreciation.

14

On my own

The Buddy Collette Quartet and Quintet

Studio work kept me busy, but jazz was always an important part of my life. After I left Chico Hamilton in 1956, I formed my own band. At first, I had a quartet with Dick Shreve on piano, John Goodman on bass, and Bill Dolney, drums. We were playing at the Haig on Wilshire Boulevard one night, when Creed Taylor, the top guy then at ABC Paramount, came in. I didn't know who he was, but I knew the name. He liked us and gave me his card: "I'm Creed Taylor and I'd like you to make me an album of your group. Just send me the tape. Send me the contracts and the amounts." That was unheard of. "Just go in a studio, do it, and send me the tape." That was beautiful.

We went in and did an album for Creed, *Calm, Cool, Collette*, that was on the ABC Paramount label. One problem was that I was also recording with Lester Koenig on Contemporary Records. I hadn't signed with either one of them, but I had just done my second record with Les, called *A Nice Day*. Both records came out about the same time and Les wasn't too happy about this.

Before I left Chico, I had already done my first album with Les. In three sessions during February and April 1956, we recorded twelve tracks for an album that would be called *Man of Many Parts*. Les wasn't completely happy with the results. He had been recording the Lighthouse bands, who played things he could understand, the West Coast Cool sound. Les really didn't know what jazz was at that time. He liked Dixieland and had become friends with Shelly Manne and a few guys, and he started recording them because he liked them. Spud Murphy had recommended me to Les as someone he should record. He finally called and asked me to bring him an album. When I told him who was on the date – Red Callender, Bill Green, Gerald Wilson, Dave Wells, Joe Comfort, Jewell Grant, Eugene Wright, Ernie Freeman – he didn't recognize any of the names. In addition, I had different music that wasn't like what he'd been getting from the Lighthouse guys, many of whom had studied with Wesley La Violette. "Jungle Pipe," for example, had a twelve-tone structure.

Poor Les. When he came into the recording session, he just couldn't get his beat going, and as the day went by his face got longer and longer. At the end of the day, he said, "I thought you were going to bring me a jazz album."

I looked at him and said, "I thought I did."

"But I didn't know any of the people and I didn't know any of the music that you played."

"Well, let's just forget it."

I knew we had some sounds there, but I was tired and just disgusted. I left and didn't call him back. After eight, ten days, Les called me. I didn't even want to hear him.

"What is it, you found something else wrong?"

"Buddy, you can record for me anytime you want."

"What are you saying?"

"I've had a chance to sit with this record, with Shelly and André [Previn]. They all said the guy's got something."

So he had a change of heart. It also helped, once he got the album out, that it got some attention, a lot of radio play, and Ralph Gleason in San Francisco wrote, "Collette's album is all one could want."

In my working band I always had four instruments on the stand with me. I was playing alto and tenor, flute and clarinet. Later on I began to play more tenor. I liked both saxes, but in the context of a small group, I felt I got more contrast between the flute, clarinet, and tenor. With the tenor it was a bigger contrast than with the alto. I play soprano now, but I don't take it on the job. Part of the reason is there are a lot of good soprano players and I'd rather have the challenge on clarinet. If I played the soprano, I probably wouldn't be playing clarinet as much. One night recently, I just had my flute and tenor on the stand and it didn't seem complete. I like to look at the clarinet, and in the course of the evening I'll figure out one tune or so to play on it. That makes me feel like a person with a complete dinner. At least I've done it. If I don't pull it out, I feel like something's missing. But three is enough! One is plenty, two is a headache, and three. ... You wonder about the person who wants to do that.

Later on I expanded to a quintet. We worked at a place called the Cellar on Hollywood Boulevard, a great jazz room in the Vermillion Hotel. Guitarist Al Viola was in the band now, Wilfred Middlebrooks on bass, Earl Palmer on drums; then we hired Gerald Wilson on trumpet. We had Gerald there because he played with us on the *Stars of Jazz* TV show hosted by Bobby Troup. We opened on a Friday at the Cellar and the *Stars of Jazz* show was on Monday. I figured, "Well, Gerald, why don't you come and play the Cellar job? Then we'll all be tight." We rehearsed at the club and the lady in charge, Terry Lester, heard us and wanted Gerald to join the band, which was great. It gave us two horns and a real good quintet. We recorded an album for Dootone, Dootsie Williams' label, called *Buddy's Best*, and one on Bel Canto Records. We did two or three shows for the *Stars of Jazz*.

We played in a lot of the clubs around Los Angeles. One good spot was the Times Restaurant on Ventura Boulevard and we played Shelly's Manne Hole. Sometimes Gerald was with us and sometimes he wasn't. We did a big concert at Loyola Marymount University in the early sixties that included George Shearing's and Dave Brubeck's groups. We had a hot group and made it tough for the other guys. Our band was very good then; it was a steaming group. We were playing all the time, so we knew what we had. Their groups were also great. George's music was more polite and Dave was still kind of polite. But you can imagine, our quintet with two horns, and Earl Palmer is a very swinging drummer, and Wilfred had played with Eric Dolphy's group before he left town. So we had a lot of energy in that band.

Even though I was busy doing studio work, my weekends – Fridays and Saturdays – would be with my groups. Al Viola and I have been playing together for about thirty-five years or more. I still use him most of the time, if he's available. Same with Gerald Wiggins. We've worked together all through the years. We did a recording with Chico Hamilton and all of the guys called *Swinging Gig*, a very good record. We had Jim Hall, Chico, Wig, John Anderson, and Curtis Counce on bass. Then we did an album with Johnny Otis and Sleepy Stein that was released as *Tanganyika*.

I seemed to be doing albums for everyone during this period. From 1956 to 1958, '59, I was in a studio almost every week. Aside from Chico and my bands, I was in sessions for Lyle "Spud" Murphy, Corky Hale, Leonard Feather, Barney Kessel, Nellie Lutcher, Jimmy Giuffre, Buddy Rich, Howard Rumsey, Red Callender, Red Norvo, Jerry Fielding, Quincy Jones, John Graas, Herbie Mann, Frank Sinatra, John Williams, Carmen McRae, Julie London, Louie Bellson, Earl Bostic, Pete Rugolo, Benny Goodman, and Benny Carter.

I did a recording for Liberty Records called *Everybody's Buddy*, for an actor named Jeffrey Hunter, as well as one for Max Albright and Motif Records. Max was a fine studio drummer and percussionist at NBC, who always wanted to play jazz. I used him on a few calls. He was a very energetic guy and was always nervous. He played great percussion, all the mallets and everything, but he'd always be talking about how many things he had to do. He'd say, "I had skates on tonight." But I knew he could handle it; he could read everything. So Max got a record date and wanted me to write some of the music for him. We helped him get a good jazz album out called *Mood for Max*, and I wrote a tune for it called "Mood for Max." He died about two years later, but he did get a chance to play jazz, which made him very happy. He was about thirty-five years old, but what a nice human being. Max Albright.

Jazz in Italy

I went to Italy for the first time in March 1961. What a trip that was. In one month I did four albums, including one with the La Scala String Quartet, composed twenty or thirty songs, did a TV show in San Remo, some movies, and many concerts. Most of what I did there was never seen or heard back here, but it was a good move to go over there. Sitting here in Los Angeles most people don't know you. When I went to Europe, naturally, I noticed the difference. They knew me.

The trip was arranged by a friend of mine over there named George Moran, who was in the wine business and was from Lodi, California. I met George in Los Angeles and he loved jazz. He had heard me play at the Cabaret Concerts on Sunset Boulevard in 1956 or 1957. He was there with his cousin, Marge, and they were two people who were having too much fun. He invited me over to his table and said, "Man, you're too good for this town."

"Well, maybe so, but what are you suggesting?"

"You've got to go to New York. You've got to go somewhere where they'll appreciate you."

I met him the next day and he was much better after he had his coffee. He invited me to stay at his home in Phoenix, where I met his family. We got to be good friends. I did a few writing projects for him and did some commercials for banks.

Then George went to Europe with his family. They were into the Royal Host Winery and he had a steady income, which enabled him to blow a lot of money. He used to call me up about every week, put all of his kids on the phone and then give me the same message: "Man, you got to come over to Europe. They love you over here."

"Yeah, but I don't have any invitations from Europe."

"Well, I'll work on it."

About two weeks later, he called back. "We've got a deal for you in San Remo, Italy, at the San Remo Jazz Festival and they will send the ticket to you."

In March 1961 I flew to Italy. George picked me up and we drove from Milan to San Remo, stopping at every pub on the way, because he loved to have his taste. I finally had to drive, in a car with the steering wheel on the right side, because George was out of it. We got to San Remo by the end of the day. I was carting him into the room when Jacques Pelzei, a saxophone player from Belgium, walked in and laughed: "You're Buddy, right? I've never seen the artist take care of a manager before!"

160

After dropping George off, I went down to the casino room and there were two guys behind the bar, who were apparently the owners or the promoters. They looked at me like they'd seen a ghost. It was the strangest feeling. When I went back to the room, George was still kind of loaded and I asked what the hell was going on, what kind of a deal did we get with these guys? He told me $250 for the trip.

"You mean the ticket and the $250?"

"They didn't send the ticket. I sent the ticket."

He never had booked anybody before and they had just quoted him a performance fee. Well, I wouldn't play for that, and George went and straightened it out with them, and got another $700 or $800. As much as George had screwed it up, it had worked out for me because I was there and I was the hit of the festival.

When they found out who I was and some of the work I had done, they put me on the half-hour TV broadcast of the festival for twenty minutes, practically the whole show. The camera was tight on me as I played flute, clarinet, and saxophone. I was working with guys who were good players: Martial Solal and Daniel Humair. The next day I felt like a star. In 1961 there weren't many channels, so most people saw me, if they were watching TV. How could you beat that? When I walked the streets after that, people would come up to me and say, "San Remo! San Remo!" I was pretty fortunate to be there and get that kind of exposure.

During that month I worked very hard, but didn't even feel it. One night at dinner I mentioned to a few of the guys that I needed a place with a piano to write. One of them offered me his music store: "You come tomorrow at twelve, because the place is closed down." The next day, after he let me in, he closed the door and his staff all went to lunch. I stayed and wrote during the lunch period. He didn't even know me. The people over there were great. Normally, with me in a store like that by myself, I would have expected cops to look in and say, "What are you doing in there?"

It was a great experience meeting a lot of the players and working with Romano Mussolini, George Joyner (who later changed his name to Jamil Nasser), and Buster Smith. George and Buster were stranded over there. They had been playing with a musician who had died suddenly. It really worked out for everyone, because they needed work and I needed a group. Romano was a jazz pianist and Benito Mussolini's son. When Chet Baker met him, he said, "Too bad about your old man." I don't know how Romano answered that.

One night, a big party was given by the Martini wine company for three of us: myself, a top opera star, and a rock star named Umberto. I'll never forget that evening with the cameras turning. We were all taking bows, having great food, and watching Miss Italy – just a fabulous evening. It was very important to do things like this, where there is appreciation. I hadn't received any of that at home. It changed my life to go to Italy and see that these people know who you are.

During one of the recording sessions in Milan, a gentleman walked in dressed very sharp, nice hat, and introduced himself: "I'm Alberto Locatelli. I know your music, and welcome to Italy. I'd like you to do something for me before you leave." He was one of the big producer guys in the country. I saw trucks running around town with "Locatelli Spaghetti" painted on them. A multi-millionaire jazz fan, Locatelli was planning a very big night with 250 of his friends to show that jazz was as important as classical music. He had gotten this theater that looked like the La Scala opera house, but it was much smaller, and very intimate. He had hired quite a few jazz artists, including Jacques Pelzei, Gianni Basso, and Oscar Valdambrini, and a bunch of other musicians who were the top players in Italy for a while. I was working in a jazz club every night with Basso and Valdambrini, and recorded an album in Milan for Ricordi with the Basso-Valdambrini Quintet.

I went to Locatelli's house the afternoon of the concert and he had this wonderful living room with a big piano and a full drum set. He had been a composition major in college. "This is my love, but at the office they think I'm crazy." His living room in this great mansion was round and the walls were cases filled with records, not books. He must have had thousands and thousands of them. He told me, "I've got everything you've ever done right here." And the concert was outstanding. He had us in tuxes; black tie; his audience also. He loved jazz so much that he wanted to show his friends what they were missing.

It was a great thing to happen to us, because Locatelli was one of the most powerful people, financially, and he helped us all so much. He was able to make the entire trip so much easier by contacting many people, and he was instrumental in setting up the record date and concert with the La Scala String Quartet. In fact, all of the record dates that we made he was always there. Many people were calling at the hotel to interview me, and they'd bring an interpreter. So for that month I was in the hands of many good friends. It was terrific. We didn't stay in touch after I left, but what Locatelli did was very inspirational, to present not just me, but the Italian musicians as well on a first-rate level.

My last record date before leaving Italy was for George Moran, my friend, who set up this tour. One day before I was to leave Italy, he told me he wanted an album. I had to write all of the music the night before and hustle the guys into the studio. George was a basket case that day. He was drinking, and beer bottles were everywhere. It's my last day and I'm trying to make some good music. We did record "Lonely Flute" and "One for the Air." I called them that because I knew that by the time we recorded those two tunes, it would be time to catch my plane. "Lonely Flute" came about because we needed another cut, and I had about another hour in the studio before I had to get to the airport. Rather than try to learn a whole piece with everybody, I decided to have the engineer just turn on the tape, and I improvised alone on my flute – one take. I played like I was in a performance, and didn't have any music. When I finished I said, "Keep that," and made a dash to the airport.

It was a great trip, all music for a month. I was getting three or four hours of sleep a night, but I didn't feel tired. I was on top of the world. I had to learn the different pacing of the Italian people and the musicians, especially when we were doing a record session. Here in LA at that time we'd do three or four tunes in three hours. There, we did one tune in three hours. When I'd try to get two, I felt they were saying, "Not until we have our break and not until we have our cappuccino," and then they'd come back. You'd get spoiled, but the product was better, because you didn't go as fast. Twenty-five years later I was doing an album in Italy with James Newton for Giovanni Bonandrini's Soul Note Records. We were doing so well for the first three hours – maybe three tunes – and then we took our break. We all went to lunch at one of those fine Italian restaurants, and spent about three hours there. Finally, I said, "Guys! we'd better get back or else we'll never finish." We had to work that night and I had to be the pushy person to get it done.

In 1961 it was just fabulous that I could go to Italy, and with nothing really set up except the San Remo gig, enjoy a month full of concerts, recordings, interviews, meeting people like Locatelli, Martini, and Ricordi, from the Ricordi Record Company. In Los Angeles you don't see the big guys very much. You see someone who's calling the signals. In Italy the big people come out of the woodwork to see you. Locatelli would leave his office saying, "I'll be at a record session. If anybody needs me, I'll call you later." It was very nice to see that. They knew what things other than money were important. I could have stayed longer.

15
Surviving the 1960s and 1970s

Studies, gigs, and calls

When I came back from Italy, I did a lot of studio work and continued to play with my jazz band. There were recording sessions with Al Hibbler, Les McCann, Gerald Wilson, Shorty Rogers, and Howard Rumsey's Lighthouse All-Stars. Then, in 1963, I went to New York to work with Ella Fitzgerald. Norman Granz, her manager, called and said Ella would like me to conduct for her. Of course, I went and was making as much money as the whole band. I bought a couple of tuxedos and decided to stay for a while; I had plenty of offers. I stayed at Charles Lloyd's apartment in Greenwich Village, at One Sheridan Square, above a theater. Charles had gone out on the road with Chico Hamilton. Eric Dolphy and I used to practice there every day.

I returned to Los Angeles in 1964 and left about five grand in the bank in New York. I was hoping to go back to live there and had returned to Los Angeles only because of the problems my ex-wife was having, and to help my kids. It was in 1964 that I legally took the kids.

When I got back home, I continued studying. I studied privately with Ernest Kanitz, who used to teach at USC, but had retired by the mid-sixties. I also studied with George Trembley who had been a student of Arnold Schoenberg. George more or less invented his own system of twelve tones with a student of his who was into computers. With Schoenberg, you use a twelve-tone row with the regular and the retrograde. You'd use the notes that you set up and then go in reverse. That was the technique he learned from Schoenberg and that's the way Schoenberg wrote. In working with his student,

George figured there's got to be more ways to set these rows up. They came up with over a hundred different arrangements of setting up the row. They figured out ways to jump over notes and start the row going down instead of across. It's very interesting. You go across with twelve notes along the top of the page; then you go down and skip over a note. That gives you a different scale. Even though it would be similar, the notes will be different. While seeming to start all over, it will always rearrange itself.

It sounds good, but it's just the idea that you can write from all this material. You have enough music to write a symphony without repeating the same row, if you didn't want to. George was outstanding with it. He was too good for the commercial music business, because George didn't want to be a background writer, composing for the movies or TV. He wanted to have his music right out there in front.

His system did work. George could actually take those rows and improvise on the piano with them. You've never heard such music. Just fabulous. I'm not saying it will sell a lot, but it would produce some very interesting sounds. I've written some music like that and I hope to write more. George asked me to write a blues in the twelve-tone style, which he said none of the students had done yet. It was very difficult, but I was able to do it. When I finally worked it out, George said, "I'm proud of you. I can hear the blues in there." We took the notes from "Basin Street Blues," picked the first six or seven notes of the tune, and then we added the other notes to finish the row.

I haven't played the piece very much, but I'd like to record it. In 1974 I played it in concert at California State University, Los Angeles, where I was teaching. The students still don't know what hit them. That piece was just different than anything else we played. At the same time, they were curious. "What is this?" After the concert Professor Robert Strassberg, a composer with wild hair and very much into the avant-garde, came up and shook my hand: "There's one number you played. That's some number. What is it?" Three or four other musicians said the same thing. Saxophonist Bob Cooper heard us play "Twelve-tone Blues" one night: "There's a piece that you just played. I don't know what that was." That was always the reaction. Most of the players that were studying with Trembley were not jazz players, although they could write some jazz.

Many of the busiest composers were coming to George, because he had something very special. Earl Hagen, Abe Most, Lalo Schifrin, and, I think, Oliver Nelson might have gone to him for a while. They were all curious: "What's this guy got?" Earl Hagen would come over the night before a picture call sometimes. George might give him a new row and show him how to do something new.

Finally, George became very depressed and it wasn't just the money. He was not being discovered. It just about drove him crazy after a while. He had achieved a very high musical stature, but where could he go? All he was doing was teaching, while the studio giants coming to him were making money and being very successful. Earl Hagen had about five shows on every week and was more or less using a lot of Trembley's method. George started drinking heavily. A couple of times, when I went for my lesson, his wife would say, "He's in bad shape today." He'd be on the floor drunk. It was pitiful. He finally fell out with his wife, and, after a while, he died.

Basically all the systems were trying to get away from relying on just the seventh and the ninth chord. All of a sudden you'd get a little rub in there or have chords that you couldn't always name. You'd come up with new ideas. Studying with people like Trembley, Schillinger, and Spud Murphy did wonders for me. It opened my mind and made me more aware of creativity and how to use it in the jazz world. The audience is waiting to hear different things; not always stuff that they don't understand, but if you can have a program that's a nice balance of different things, you can slip one in. That's what I did with the twelve-tone piece, and that's what I did with "Blue Sands."

During this time, I was continuing to compose and arrange. In 1964 I arranged four pieces for Thelonious Monk, when he was at the Monterey Jazz Festival. Mingus was at that Festival also, with a bigger group. Jimmy Lyons, the promoter, figured that since he was bringing musicians from Los Angeles to work with Mingus, why not also add them to Monk's quartet. Mingus was working on Saturday, and Monk on Sunday. Jimmy said, "Why don't you arrange something for Monk and we'll use him as an octet." I said, "Fine." Jimmy sent me Monk's music and I arranged four pieces.

When we got there, we did Mingus' job and then had to rehearse with Monk. We kept running over his music and Monk wouldn't sit at the piano; he just kept standing around, looking a little confused and unhappy. Then Charlie Rouse, his saxophonist, who was sitting there and playing the music also, said, "Monk likes everything very short." So I went over to the guys and said, "Play everything short." We had been playing "Straight, No Chaser" smoothly, and then we switched to a more staccato approach. As we got into it, Monk smiled and went over to the piano and played with a lot of feeling. But he couldn't say, "I don't like it." Charlie saved us, and we went on stage and broke it up. That was a great weekend, excellent festival, two days back-to-back with the two giants of that period – Mingus and Monk.

Then it was back to Los Angeles with gigs, studio calls, and record dates. There were Frank Sinatra albums and working with Nat Cole, who was doing a lot of albums and had his own show, *The Nat King Cole Show*. I played with Louie Bellson, and Stan Kenton in his Neophonic Orchestra, doing his recording sessions and performances of Wagner's music. I was a very busy studio musician and I still had my jazz quintet on weekends. We gigged around LA and regularly played a club in La Jolla, near San Diego, called the Pour House.

I scored a movie in 1961 called *Trauma*. It wasn't a jazz thing; it was a suspense movie, and that was my first big score. I composed all original music, sixty minutes in a ninety-minute film. The movie was not too good and the people behind it knew it. When they approached me to do the score they told me, "We hope the music can save the film." Well, the music can never save a bad film and mine didn't, but I was satisfied with the music. It turned out well, and people said nice things about the score.

The music did create a terrifying atmosphere. Marty Butler, a good composer, told me that he saw the movie late one night and the music frightened him to death. I had to work hard to get that feeling. At this time I was playing in the Los Angeles production of *Gypsy*, which had a very different kind of score, much more upbeat. I'd come home and have to somehow get in the frame of mind to compose for *Trauma*. I'd turn the heat up, wouldn't shave, would let the piano cover fall on my hands. I had to find some way to turn myself into a madman and it actually worked! If someone telephoned during those times, I'd just snarl at them and hang up. You couldn't be Mister Nice Guy and compose music for a film like that.

In 1969 I was the director of a festival called "Jazz by the Bay," in San Diego. Sammy Davis and Herbie Hancock were there. I had the big band with a reed section of Bill Green, Jackie Kelson, Dave Sherr, John Baimbridge, and Plas Johnson. Bobby Bryant and Fred Hill were on trumpets; Red Callender played bass and tuba, and Joe Sample was on piano. We had a dynamite group and a lot of original music.

I was also playing clubs up and down the west coast, but the jazz scene had changed during the 1960s and 1970s in Los Angeles. The music had changed; there was a lot of rock 'n' roll, and fusion was coming in. The clubs cut back on jazz and not a lot was happening for jazz musicians in the United States. It was good that I was doing a lot of studio work, because it was very, very tough for jazz music. Even when we'd play clubs, no one was writing anything about it. There was very little inspiration from the record companies. Many musicians decided to focus just on the studios to try and make some money, to try to stay busy, and to survive.

In the studio with Duke

I went to Japan in 1966 with Percy Faith, who had one of the better bands I've ever played with, including strings. Percy took all the top players from LA. Not too many of us had been to Japan before and we all went for the first-time experience. I was the only black in the band, out of forty-five people. We did a three-week tour, which was great. Japan was quite different than it is now. It wasn't nearly as expensive and everything was quite small, like the apartments and the beds. You could hardly get into the bathrooms. I had to duck my head.

I saw Duke Ellington over there. Actually, before I left with Percy Faith, I had done a movie with Duke Ellington for Paramount called *Assault on the Queen*. Frank Sinatra got him to do the picture and Duke wrote a lot of great music for it. Duke was about 70 years old then and felt that he hadn't been treated fairly in Hollywood. During one of the sessions, as we talked, he said, "Well, they wanted Duke. I'm going to give them Duke."

He added Bud Shank and I to do some flute parts. We didn't play much saxophone, maybe a little. I guess Duke felt that he would lighten up the score a little with a flute solo. They also added Murray McEachern, who was a fine trombone player. The music was so great and the band was screaming. To be in that band and hear how they played was something special. There were nuances that came only from years of teamwork. Bud Shank and I were in between a couple of Duke's guys, and we kept looking at each other and saying, "What's going on here?" We couldn't figure it out. As we played, we'd feel the whole stand vibrate. We'd want to hang on; it's an earthquake! Well, the overtones would set up the way those guys played and they could do that. The air's going in the right place and all that, boy! I mean, there's a lesson within itself. What can you tell anyone? You just have to be there.

The band recorded one thing for the saxes and we were a part of that. Murray was one of those musicians that could play any instrument and write. He was so scary, almost too good, if you can imagine that. He played trombone, trumpet, alto sax – trombone like Tommy Dorsey and alto like Johnny Hodges. He might not have played the alto for seven or eight months; he'd put it in his mouth and it would come out so perfectly. The reed might even have been dry. And he had that professor look that said, "You mean this is supposed to be hard?" Well, that's the kind of guy he was. Murray looked at Duke's sixteen bars for the reeds that we had just played and said, "Now, I can see what's written here, but there's something else coming out of the horns." It was baffling. We heard the difference, but we didn't know how it happened.

Another thing I noticed was how there was control, but also lack of control in the band, if I can explain it that way. Duke's the leader;

he knew what he was going to get, but at the same time it seemed that he wasn't leading. He wrote out some triplets and things that were very hard, because it was going to be fast and it ran through all the registers of your horn. The band said, "Duke, this is too difficult!" He laughed, didn't say yes or no, just walked away and talked with the ladies in the studio. That was his personality. In the meantime the band knew they had to play it and were trying to work it out so they wouldn't feel embarrassed.

"Man, this ain't going to work!"

"Well, you guys will figure it out."

You weren't going to get Duke upset about anything. He was riding on a cloud. So they got it and he said, "Okay, let's make a take." Now they were nervous, but these guys were so good. It wasn't that they can play everything in sight, but that they knew how to play things so they wouldn't sound bad. That's an artistic thing nobody teaches, but I've learned to do it. I've been in a lot of reed sections in the studio. They would have played it, but they wouldn't have gotten the effect that Duke's band got, because everybody would have been playing every note. When Duke's band played it, there was some stuff in there that they didn't play, which made the accents come off. The writers who were there – many of them came down to hear Duke's band – came over to see what it was. They'd say, "Well, how would you write that?" Duke was smiling, almost as if he knew, "If I write this, I'll get something else." You don't always get what you think when you write. And what he got was actually better than what it looked like.

A lot of players will try to pin you down: "How can we do this? Should we accent here?" Duke's guys didn't go through that. These guys pulled it out, because they knew that they had to make it sound good and they all somehow covered. Their teamwork did it. The clarinet was in the throat tones register and might have had a much softer sound, but it's still unison, and he had enough instruments on the parts so it didn't sound as though they were having trouble playing it. When you'd listen to it, you might say, "Man, there was great voicing there." And Duke was smiling, while everyone else was saying, "What an effect!"

We did a lot of beautiful music. The band was cooking. There was always a lot of excitement in the studio. Many of the big Hollywood writers and composers were there, because they knew Duke and wanted to find out, "How does his band do that?"

About three weeks later I got a call back to Paramount, and they were doing some of the same music again, but with a smaller orchestra and different orchestrators doing the writing. I asked around and they said, "We had to do a lot of the music over, because when we projected it with the picture, it was too strong." There was dialogue and the band would be screaming. So they rerecorded a lot of the music. Duke left them with a good score and they couldn't handle it in the picture. They didn't allow his music to come in like it could have. I made two other sessions for that picture with different orchestrators using just a few clarinets, flutes and strings on Duke's themes. It was depressing.

Duke wasn't that surprised. They paid him big money. He wasn't going to do just background music. That's what he meant when he said, "They wanted Duke. I'm going to give them Duke." He didn't back away. "If the movies are going to wait until I'm seventy-five years old and then call me to do a film, I'm going to give them me."

When we played in Japan with Percy Faith, in 1966, I told Percy one night that Duke Ellington was in the audience. Percy said, "Oh, fine." I thought he'd announce it, but he never did. Percy would usually play three numbers together like a medley and then stop for the next tune. Duke would stand up and applaud after each number, and all the Japanese would stand up: "Oh, bravo!" Duke was that kind of guy. He appreciated everyone and everything. Throughout the concert I thought, "Percy's got to say, 'Well, the wonderful Duke Ellington is in the house.'" He didn't say anything; he probably figured he was bigger than Duke. He had been a very big guy at CBS and maybe never really accepted the man. But Duke was cheering him on, and that was the way Duke was with most people. As big as he was, he'd listen to everyone. He'd come up to musicians: "I heard a little flute thing you were playing the other day." Then he came backstage and greeted everyone.

I talked to Duke about the film. He asked what happened, and I told him they pulled his score and did some reorchestrating with a small band. "I knew they were going to do that," he said. "But why did they miss the tempos I left them?" He knew already and he was right. When he told me that, I could see he was a master; a master teacher, a master everything. Isn't that a classic? But that's the scene.

After that concert, some of us went to an after-hours spot that was the hangout for musicians and artists. Thelonious Monk was there, and Jimmy Rowles, who was the piano player with Percy Faith, Joe Mondragon, Gene Cipriano, and some of the other band members. Jimmy had never met Thelonious Monk, and said he'd love to meet him. Since I knew Monk from the Monterey Jazz Festival, I told Jimmy I'd introduce him. We walked over to Monk, who had his hat on and was bouncing and turning around a little bit.

"Monk, this is Jimmy Rowles. He's a fine piano player from LA. He knows your work, enjoys you and wanted to meet you."

"Oh, yeah, I'm really happy to see you, Monk."

And Monk said, "Yeah." Then he spun around and looked up at Jimmy: "Do you have any kids?"

Jimmy said, "Yes."

He spun around again. Jimmy was kind of befuddled. "How old?" Monk asked the second time around.

"Twenty-four."

He still didn't react, but spun around again. "Too old."

That was the conversation between Jimmy Rowles and Monk.

1965 – Watts and the Academy Awards

The year before our Japanese tour, the Watts riots erupted. I hadn't lived there in a long time, but it changed my thinking to see places that you knew well burning on TV. It wasn't a movie set; this was for real. I grew up in Watts and lived out in Compton on 123rd Street, when my kids were very young. We had a house out there. The markets were pretty bad, but that was all you had. It seemed that the Watts area was going downhill and people were frustrated in many ways. No work, and nothing was happening. There was no future.

At this same time we were trying to get more work for black musicians in Los Angeles. We had a group that used to meet at Ernie Freeman's house. In these meetings we began to see that only a few black musicians – guys like Bill Green, Plas Johnson, Earl Palmer and Red Callender – were working on a steady basis, maybe a record date here, a studio call there. Although I had finished with Groucho, there were jobs with Nelson Riddle and Billy May.

In trying to find out how many blacks were working, we asked around and couldn't see that anyone was working very much. We checked the studios to see how many they'd hired. The studios and contractors didn't like that and the musicians' union wasn't very helpful. Later in the early 1970s, some of us went through the union contracts and made a list of who was working and who was not. It was a very sad picture. Blacks were on 1 percent of all the jobs that were done; women had about 3 percent. It was a terrible picture. We went through a thousand contracts in about two or three weeks. We thought it was bad, but this showed it was worse.

When we started meeting in the sixties our attitude was healthier, more upbeat. Things were changing, and we wanted to share our experiences and find out how many musicians were working. A lot weren't, and whenever we had a meeting with contractors and some white leaders, they would all say, "Yeah, we don't know any of the other guys and we can't take a chance."

We'd say, "Well, we can make lists to make sure that the good players are here."

We started a workshop to train players, to make sure that if they got called they would be ready. But as many lists as we made out and passed along, it didn't happen.

Nineteen-sixty-five was an interesting year, not only for Watts. I remember the date because someone at one of our meetings asked if the Academy Awards had ever hired any blacks. Everyone was dumbfounded. Out of twenty-five musicians sitting in a big house, no one could think of anyone. None of us had ever done it; we figured no one ever had, and this was the thirty-seventh season. We decided to get some help from CORE. We told them what the problem was and that we wanted someone to look into the Academy Awards show.

174

CORE's Don White got in touch with John Green, the music director of the Awards. Don approached it very lightly, asking for a meeting with Green to get some publicity on the show. They scheduled a luncheon and then Don asked his first question: "Have you ever hired any blacks in the orchestra?" John Green just about choked on his salad. He wasn't quite prepared for this and the question threw him. He'd probably never thought about it.

"Well, I don't think so, and I'm pretty sure I would know if we had."

It soon became clear that if he didn't hire some blacks, the Awards would be picketed. Afterwards, Don met with us again and told us that John Green would definitely find somebody, and that he already knew some names.

Bill Green, a lady named Toni Robinson, who was a black harpist, and myself were called for the upcoming Academy Awards, and it was history-making. We got to the rehearsal and people were excited, probably because many of them knew Bill and me. There was Ted Nash, Gene Cipriano, and Ronnie Lang. So the rehearsals went well. Naturally, Bill and I could blend in with everyone. John was very nervous because he still thought that there would be problems, but there was no picketing or anything like that. I think the word got out that we were hired, and that cooled everything down.

We were curious about something else when we saw how the evening developed. This was the year after Sidney Poitier won the Best Actor Oscar for *Lilies of the Field*. That was a big event, and we thought about it later on. There was so much strategy being played that evening and some degree of pressure. People connected with the Academy were shaking in their boots and were hoping that blacks weren't going to say that they were treated unfairly. The Academy couldn't have that. I'm not saying Sidney Poitier wasn't great, but the timing was really important for us, and that seemed like a big turnaround. We felt, "Wow! Things are better than we thought. If he can win, then maybe some of us are well off." Of course, no black has since won Best Actor. There's no way to know, because nobody will ever say. But I think that for them it was the right move to make at the time to quell all of that discontent.

There was something else that made me suspicious about that night. I was seated purposely on the outside of the orchestra, right next to the audience, where the camera would pick me up. The cameraman almost knocked my head off a couple of times. I got calls and letters from friends in New York: "Man, they were showing you like crazy! You must be the star!" I began to see their plan. Part of it was to let people know that there were some blacks in the orchestra. Therefore, "Don't do any picketing or bombing." And at that time they were really frightened.

That evening threw a lot of us. For a long time blacks felt that the game wasn't going to be fair. Now there was some hope, and it looked for a while like things were going to be great, but nothing changed. There were three blacks in the band: Bill, Toni and me, and that went on for about three years, until I began to feel that I was being used, and got fed up. We never worked with a lot of those people on any other jobs. I didn't try to influence Bill or Toni, but I was into a lot of activities and fighting a lot of little battles at that time, and helping the ACLU. I met a lot of people who were fighters and tried to weigh things. Someone would ask, "Are you guys still doing the Academy Awards?" I would answer, "Yes, the same three and it's going to stay that way."

The next time Bobby Helfer, the contractor, called me to do the Academy Awards, I said, "Bobby, I can't do it this time." He couldn't understand that, because it's a prestige job; you don't say no. But that was it as far as I was concerned. "I feel that each year it's going to be just three people, and I'm going to do something else this time." I really took a chance, because you can blow your career in a thing like that. Bobby was the biggest and the most powerful contractor in town; he could ruin you. But I'm fighting, and every now and then you've got to let them know what you feel. Bobby did hire another black in my place, a bass player. So they still had three.

Leonard Feather called me and Bobby Helfer, and told Bobby, "You've got three people again. I thought you'd hire more." Bobby said, "We would have had four, but Buddy Collette turned me down." How about that! He turned it around and Leonard wrote it up that way: "They would have had four, but Buddy turned him down." Then people came and asked, "Well, why did you turn him down?" Some said I blew it, because I didn't take the job. But I knew if I had been there, it still would have been three. This time black musicians did picket, but it wasn't very effective, and it stayed with just three people for a long time.

We were able to put pressure on certain people and it did eventually change. When Quincy Jones first did the Awards, it was about half and half with blacks and whites. Usually there might have been five or six minorities in an orchestra of forty or fifty, and many times none. The days of pointing out these things and fighting seem over for now, and you figure if people don't work together and try to use the best players, no matter what color they are, then we're missing a lot in life.

Back into network TV

I did manage to stay busy in the studios during the sixties and eventually got back into network TV. I began doing *The Danny Kaye Show* in 1967. That was the first steady show I had done since Groucho Marx. We had two blacks on that show; Red Callender and me. Paul Weston was the leader, and he was a good guy to work for. He liked us and the way we played. Red and I stayed with the show for a few years. The only problem was that we didn't make that much money, but we got a lot of overtime because of Danny and his work habits. In 1958, I had done the *Swinging Shepherds* album with Harry Klee, Bud Shank, and Paul Horn, the four flutes, and a rhythm section of Joe Comfort, Bill Miller, and Bill Richmond. I gave a copy to Paul Weston, who got very excited about it and did one of the numbers from the album "Tasty Dish" on Danny's show.

When that show went off, I was hired for *The Carol Burnett Show*. The music director was Harry Zimmerman. Red Callender and Plas Johnson were in the band, so we had three blacks. I was playing lead alto and Red was playing tuba and bass. Harry wanted Plas there because he was a very good tenor player. Harry was a good guy and he knew who he wanted: "I've got to have you and you." We had a good band and we got along. I stayed there for a couple of years, until the show dropped Harry and hired Peter Matz.

Harry was a good writer, but some felt he wrote the old school style. He was an older guy and did write a lot of busy notes. He had played some organ in silent movie theaters and places like that, and Harry wrote that way for the band. By 1969 things were changing. Rock 'n' roll was coming in everywhere and the bands had to change their format. They weren't doing those notey, radio-type sounds anymore. The kind of writing that Harry did was out. CBS brought Peter Matz in, and they didn't tell Harry that he'd been fired. One day he drove up to his parking stall and saw that his name had been painted off.

Peter Matz brought in his band from New York and one thing led to another. It was time for a change. I had been at CBS for four or five years, first with *Danny Kaye* and then right into *Carol Burnett*. In 1970 I went to NBC to work with leader George Wyle on *The Flip Wilson Show*. He had a few more black musicians in his band: Al Aarons and Grover Mitchell, who were just out of Count Basie's band, as well as Red, Bill Green, Ronnell Bright (piano player), and me. That was the most blacks hired in Los Angeles on a steady show. There were ten or twelve white players in the band. I don't know if Flip Wilson ever said that there should be a certain number of blacks in the band, but George probably anticipated that. It was a swinging band and most of the guys played solos. George would write numbers for us to open the show with and would feature different guys during the show. It was real family.

I want to credit those leaders who were responsible for hiring minority talent and sticking by their judgment; people such as Jerry Fielding, Paul Weston, Harry Zimmerman, George Wyle, and John Parker. In the recording studios there were Billy May and Nelson Riddle. Red Mandel, saxophonist and contractor, was also good at hiring black musicians. He later did *The Sonny and Cher Comedy Hour*, *The Smothers Brothers Show*, and *The Danny Kaye Show*.

Controlling our music

Another thing a few of us did in the sixties was to establish our own publishing company, called Marcel Publishing, which is my middle name. We were all writing our own music and the record companies always wanted to publish your work. That means giving half of the tune away to them. The royalties on your tunes would go to the record company first, and then they would send you your share. So we got together in 1965 and hired a lawyer, who was part of the company, to help take care of the business and to protect our rights and royalties. Ernie Freeman, John Anderson, and Curtis Counce, a bass player, were all part of it. It was a Broadcast Music, Inc. (BMI) company, formed to protect our music. Later on, we all got our own companies. Each of us began an American Society of Composers, Authors, and Publishers (ASCAP) company. Mine is called Veda Music.

A few years later, around 1972, 1973, some of us working *The Flip Wilson Show* – Grover Mitchell, Red Callender, Al Aarons, and myself – decided to form our own record company. We wanted to protect our tunes and get our albums out there. There was a guy named Walt Sage, who was part of this, and an English guy named Pat Boyle, who was here trying to promote. So we all met, agreed, and got a license. We called ourselves Legend Records, because we were all legends at the time. We had a studio out in the San Fernando Valley, where we could rehearse and record. The idea was that each would be a leader and do an album using the rest of us, who would donate our services. About five or six of us did that, including Leroy Vinnegar and Al Viola, who did a solo album. My album was called *Now and Then*. The title tune was written by Pat Boyle, who also handled distribution for us. We ultimately had about eight or ten albums. But Pat was not sharing the money with the guys, and he had put his name on everything. We were all very busy and left most of the business end in his hands. When we found out what was going on, Pat couldn't be found. Even his wife said she had no idea where he was. It was a sad day.

We more or less dissolved Legend Records. Everyone was so busy that no one had the time to get into the business end, much less straighten this mess out. But we learned a lot and a little while later, Red Callender, Grover Mitchell, and myself established RGB (R[ed]G[rover]B[uddy]) Records. We put a few more albums out, but didn't really have the time to do more than that.

16
Passing on the magic

Teaching

In the early forties, if you had a different sound and could play, leaders would look for you. People wanted a fresh approach. I hope we haven't lost that. One of the reasons I'm enjoying my teaching role, and I always have, is because I help students have confidence about what they do and be proud of what they've got. I'm also aware of how important it is, because the greatest thing now is to catch some of us that are around and have us teach. We had this when we were growing up. Today's students don't have this. They have all the technology, the computers, the films, and the archives, but people like Chico and I are still telling the stories on the instruments rather than with words. This is valuable and we're here to tell it. I feel like a messenger, because whether it's Mingus or Duke or Basie, whoever you want to talk about, we can talk about because we were with them. They're not here to do it, that's the *only* sad part.

When I was in junior high school we had a program from the Works Progress Administration (WPA) and, would you believe? Lester Young, the great tenor player, and people like that would come to our schools. So we had the chance to make these acquaintances and to talk to them. They would tell us what to do, how to be a good musician, get a teacher, get a good instrument, and all that.

Nowadays the students are drawing from records and TV, and radio, but you have to meet the musicians in person; you really do. That's when it changes. If you see a youngster, twenty years old, who's playing good, you might think that he's going to be famous. Well, that just doesn't happen. We have to take them from that spot, when they have that spark, and move them to the next level. I got a lot of help from people like Mr. Paul Howard, who was the secretary of the black union on Central Avenue. He knew my parents, and when I was twelve or thirteen, he'd always warn me, "Don't get into that dope," or, "Don't do this or do that." He told me some things that were very helpful at a time when I wasn't even worried about getting into trouble.

That's why with the teaching we are doing now, when we see them growing every week, we talk to them and we help them solve some of their problems. We feel sometimes like we are their parents, because there are little things that we catch, and there are a lot of things that they need. So what can you do except try to help them, 'cause that's going to make a better world for all of us.

James Newton, flutist, was the same kind of young man as Eric Dolphy. He came to me with rough skills, twenty years old. He'd been studying with Miles Zentner of the Los Angeles Philharmonic.

"Since Miles doesn't play jazz, he said come and see you."

"Well, let's see what we can do with you." James played well. I just said, "Here are some things that we can do to smooth you out, center your tone a little bit, let you hear the difference." We played duets and intervals together. You listen, watch your time, and then you're on your way to being a good musician.

James' first record wasn't too good. He and the guitar player weren't in tune, but this is what you need the most, the guidance. When we played together, I could find out if I felt comfortable with him as a team player. I'm not talking about his talent for solo playing. When you have the blend between the two flutes happening, you say, "Hey, I'll see you down the line somewhere. There's nothing much I can tell you."

Some students come here and want to do one thing so much that they don't care about the other things.

I'd say, "When we played together, the intonation...."

"Look, I'm going to have my own band anyway and I want to be a soloist."

"Yeah, but that's a long road." You don't want to say, "Well fine, then why did you come?" Most of those guys you never see anymore, because they're not going to be able to work on the things that will help them. It's not just your personality. It's the way you sound; it's the way you can accept whatever part and be a team player. Some of these tips I was able to pass on to a few players that, I'm happy to say, made it.

In 1973 I started teaching at California State University at Los Angeles. I was very busy at the time with shows and recordings. But when they called and said they wanted me, I was intrigued by the idea of teaching, so I took the job. After rehearsals at night with the students, we'd go to some of the student hangouts – Bob's Big Boy and the Little Bear Parlor – so they could ask questions and talk – not always about music, but who's in the business, who do I know, what do they do and what are they like. We'd be up until midnight sometimes. It was enjoyable answering the questions of these young minds that wanted to know about jazz. I kept thinking that this is the part of teaching that's mostly missing. Some of those players that were at Cal State Los Angeles made it pretty big, and the questions about the business part, the lifestyles, the personalities, were very important. I would take the class to jobs with me so they could see what we were doing – blending, being team players, matching with this person, being flexible, all those things. When I began to talk later about the job and the session they had been to, they could see more of what it all meant.

"Oh, I see, then you had to play softer because you were not playing the lead, right?"

"If the lead player's playing soft, don't overplay, because that will get you fired. It's not your band."

The musicians, who were most flexible, were in demand. "We need a little jazz, eight-bar chorus here, real hot." "Now we need a little Latin flute on this one." And you have to shift gears. To many of the students this was amazing. They tended to put everyone in one category. "Well, he plays jazz alto, and that's it." But that was what I was teaching at the college. That's why some of those same players are very busy today. It's like being a carpenter; you've got to take a couple more tools with you, because you may need a drill or an extra hammer. I think the student should be taught that.

A lot of the players in the jazz scope want to be soloists, great studio players like Ernie Watts or David Sanborn. They're soloists that come in and make big money, which is great. But the teamwork approach is the best approach for a successful career. You also have to get around, meet people, do the legwork, make rehearsals, and hope that the contractor will call you and that you impress him, when you read the parts. There's a lot to learn, but most is done with lessons, practice at home, and getting into rehearsal situations. Going out and listening is important, because other than that, you won't know what you're practicing for. I think teachers who are not active, teach something that's good, but not necessarily something that's going to be useful when a student goes for a job.

I stayed at Cal State LA four years and enjoyed it, because it was a learning experience for me, a chance to grow, develop and find out what kind of teacher I was in the classroom. I had cut down on the number of private students to just a few and I continued to teach privately, but college was a different experience. I subsequently spent a year on the faculty at Cal State, Dominguez Hills, and four years at Loyola Marymount University, as musical director of their jazz workshop. During the 1992/93 academic year I was at California State Polytechnic Institute at Pomona, conducting the jazz band.

Recently, a group of musicians and I have been teaching young students and playing music at middle and high schools – and not always for money – something similar to the workshops we used to have; to make it a better music business for the new players. In 1994, I helped establish Jazz America, a summer teaching program directed at the youth, that has taken off over the years and is now a corporation. Initially, I worked with Michael O'Daniel and Valerie Fields to establish a program that would bring together high school-age students with experienced local musicians like Gerry Wiggins, Ndugu Chancler, Bobby Bryant, Bill Green, John Stephens, Richard Simon, and Washington Rucker, to give the kids the training they need to become good musicians. We've continued the program each summer since then. We try to teach all aspects of musicianship, but the greatest thing about Jazz America is that we also teach them how to play together: small bands, section work, and big bands. It prepares them to be in the professional world.

But it's hard to do; you have to create that. That's why I try to surround myself with people who are positive, and who want to play and who teach and still love it. This gives you a big boost. I've been on the board of directors of the American Federation of Musicians, Local 47, for quite a few years now, and one of my goals is to try and establish something where musicians will work together, and work with new players. One way we've tried to promote this, and other goals as well, is by establishing a recording studio at the union available to all members. It's another way of getting people playing together.

In 1996 I was appointed the Executive Director of the California Institute for the Preservation of Jazz, housed at Cal State University, Long Beach. The Institute could be a lot more than just an archive, but people seem to want to turn it into that. So I can't get too excited. It's not bad to collect the old stuff, but I think it should be a facility to help young musicians today, to bring them together with the older players to communicate and learn. We should have facilities like a recording studio for these young people to perform and record their music.

I also joined their music faculty for two years as professor in charge of the jazz band, as well as teaching improvisation. When I first started I didn't have a chance to audition the players for the Number One band, which was too bad because it was not very racially diverse. Their audition was essentially just an extremely difficult reading exercise. I asked them why they were doing that, because I also had to know if they could solo and what their attitude was. My thing was to find people we could build with and not just have these intense readers. Their training was more in a classical vein. They could all read very well, and they sounded great, but they tended to be too straight, not much jazz involved, and the soloists were playing too many notes. I told them I was trying to follow their stories, but I just wasn't getting it. I wanted to take them back to Ellington and Basie, and help them learn how to swing.

I'm encouraging students, more than teaching them, to write their own melodies, and it's always a surprise for them. Sometimes they don't like what they've written. I say to them, "Well, this could be good. Take it back and work the chords a little better," or "Let's change the tempo." Some of their material is actually quite good. How else are they going to learn that, unless they want to start as bandleaders and go through the struggle.

Today, too many musicians would rather play something someone else has already played. You've got to have your own material; suppose someone does like your tune that might not yet be that strong. I think working like that gives them a lot of confidence. If someone tells them, "I like what you do," and they say, "Well, I didn't think it was that great," well, who's to judge? They might continue writing their own music with that kind of acceptance and encouragement.

Performing and recent projects

I went back to Europe in 1988 and I did some concerts with James Newton, Geri Allen on piano, and Jaribu Shahid on bass. We did the album called *Flute Talk* for Soul Note Records in Milan, and I did a live album in Sorgues, France, with some French musicians, including Andre Jaume. The whole tour was very exciting.

After that tour I realized that this was the way I'd like to travel. I don't mean like Sweets Edison, who's out there three months at a time, and home one month. I'd rather go out once or twice a year for a month or two and then concentrate on things in the States, like recordings, concerts, and teaching. It's a good schedule. It gives me a chance to practice, to work, and to just have time to spend with my family.

During that 1988 tour a guy from Verona, Nicola Tesitore, called me over and asked, "Who else do you think could come over here that the people would like?" I suggested we call Chico Hamilton and see if we could get the old group back together, which was an outstanding group. When I returned home, I called Chico. He wasn't sure if he wanted to do it. I said, "Well, you're going to make some good money, for one thing." And we did. We went over there the next year, and doing two concerts a week, we made more money than I've ever made, and more money than he's ever made working jobs. We were paid like the Modern Jazz Quartet.

When we got to The Hague, they wanted me to play with other groups. So I played with a Dutch band that works at their radio station. I also worked with six tenors, including Billy Mitchell, George Adams and a couple of Dutch guys. And I played with Bob Brookmeyer and Sy Tufts. The promoter had me going, which I didn't mind, because each setting was beautiful, the hall was always packed, and I was getting a chance to show my versatility playing with all the different groups, as well as with Chico. But there again, I was picking up two grand each time I played. So we did quite well.

The studio is great, but it's nothing like working before a live audience. When you're playing that much in front of an audience, your instrument feels right and the appreciation is fantastic. There's something that comes together that I can't explain, but you know you were there. The people are interviewing you and the cameras are snapping and they're asking you, "Can we pick you up tomorrow at the hotel?" You're on top of the world! So when you've felt that, you come home and understand what it's all about, what some of the reasons are for you devoting time to composing and practicing. There's an appreciation out there and that's the incentive we all need.

During 1985 I got my music books out: *The Buddy Collette Songbook* and *Man of Many Parts: A Discography of Buddy Collette*. Coen Hofmann from Amsterdam put them together and published them. The *Songbook* is in two volumes, about eighty tunes. Rather than me writing much new material now, I'm getting with those tunes again. I play a lot of them and there are times when a new arrangement of some of those tunes can do wonders, because the more I get exposure with my playing, the material is also getting exposure. While I was in Amsterdam, I played a tune I wrote for one of my daughters called "Crystal." Clark Terry ran over after the rehearsal and said, "Man, what was that tune that you just played? Was that yours?" He asked for a copy of it and I gave it to him. I don't know whether he recorded it, but that's the way things start.

I formed my big band in 1990, and did an inaugural concert at El Camino College in May of that year. I brought in some interesting, original music. Since I write quite a bit of original music, I find that I play more of my tunes on a concert than songs of other composers. If nothing more, the audience hears some music for the first time. I like it that way, and maybe that's where I am going most of the time, doing what many composers did before, like Ellington, Mingus, and Monk, who were playing and recording their own original music. Miles did a lot of his own compositions. We shouldn't just keep doing arrangements of things that have been done many times, or only music of people who are gone. We should spend more time on our own music and the music of those who are here now. We shouldn't have to draw only from Miles' material, play Mingus' charts, or play Monk's music. If we do, then we are stopping some of the creative processes.

I hope that more musicians will write something and say, "Well, this is my original called 'Betsy Lee' or 'One Jump Hop.'" You're better off trying a new lick and putting that out, if you've got an audience. And that's what I did at El Camino. That's what I do in all my concerts. It was so effective with the Chico Hamilton Quintet, the Stars of Swing, and on most of my albums. When I go to Europe, some fans will bring my albums and they'll be humming some of the tunes that I never knew would be popular. It does work. It starts with an idea from the head and the heart. You put it down and say, "I hope someone will like this one day." And when it comes back to you five, ten years later, there it is . . . and what a feeling!

Jazz is a getting together of all kinds of people and sharing ideas. In my big band there are some women; many races are represented and it's like one family. Jazz is very creative, which means that it allows everyone in it to communicate, to work together as a team. When you get a good group, there can be nothing better than that. But it takes a long time to understand the music and play it well.

I've been fortunate in having a good group of friends for most of my life. So when I was called, in 1996, by Patricia Willard of the Library of Congress to do a concert in Washington, DC with the big band, and compose a new piece of music for it, I had the perfect inspiration, and wrote about, and for, my long-time friends. Pat and I had talked for years about doing a concert. She used to live in Los

Angeles and knows the history of the music here and the people who are still doing it. It took about eight to ten years to make it happen, but during the first week in June of 1996 they focussed on Los Angeles and featured Benny Carter's band, Gerald Wilson's band, and my band, each performing on a different evening in a three-day series of big band concerts. The three of us were also commissioned to write original pieces. Benny wrote a piece about Martin Luther King and Gerald did a composition based on Gershwin's music.

As the planning moved ahead for the concert, I still wasn't quite sure what to call my piece. Pat asked about it and I told her that I was writing a suite about all my friends that would be playing in the band: Jackie Kelson, Chico Hamilton, Gerry Wiggins, Fred Katz, Britt Woodman. I just kept thinking about all the people I had known for fifty, sixty years. As we talked, we put the title together: *Friendships Suite: Sixty Years of Musical Togetherness*. This was my opportunity to keep the story honest about our music, about our lives.

I could see the musicians' faces as the notes went down, just jumped onto the paper, different than ever before. I could hear how each player would sound and would inspire the others. It was all about bringing people together. I wanted to feature each of my friends in the *Suite*. Gerry Wiggins is featured on "Just Another Day for Love." "Mr. and Mrs. Goodbye" was written for Jackie Kelson. I knew the kind of emotion in that very simple melody, and I wanted to share that side of Jackie with people who may not know him. He fell in love with the piece, and he did a beautiful introduction and ending on it. It just touches me when I hear it.

The concert was a dream come true. Someone from the Library of Congress came up to me and said, "This is going to be different, before you even play one note." Just being on stage together was an emotional, exciting, fantastic moment. It was a love thing and we pulled everyone into it. There was something in that hall that was so special.

Reflections on a career and a life

Looking back through all of my experiences, music has been so important to me for many reasons. Of course, I love it and I've always wanted to be the best I could be. The greatest thing has been to be able to do something I was sincere and passionate about, that I believed in. I didn't have to change anything. I've always done music. I've always taught, whether they paid me or not. I practiced, whether they paid me or not. When you're doing what you really enjoy and it finally begins to pay off, then you're ahead of the game. Sure I had to be flexible, a little bit of this, a little teaching, travel a little bit, little jobs out, studios, saxes, clarinets, flutes – the works. But basically, there was a music tag on everything. And you finally convince everyone and yourself, too, that you can do this, because there's nothing else you know like this! And that's what happened.

I don't think you realize greatness. If you do realize that, you don't reach for it. I never look for what's going to happen later. You just do the best you can now and you accept what's happening. Charles Mingus never realized that big things would happen for him. He knew he had talent and he worked harder than most people would, because he loved doing it. He did exactly the same, years later, when people knew who he was. He'd be on the piano all day and he'd be writing music, then asking, "Hey, when can we rehearse? I've got some new stuff." Where does this drive come from? A lot of people would say to him, "Boy, you've been doing that for three hours. Why don't you stop?" Well, what else can you do? I think you create your own situation, you make your own luck. Because if you're that sold on what you are doing and you're convincing people, "This is who I am," they begin to believe that that's who you are. And there it is. That's the energy, the ideas, the kind of drive you need to become not just a Mingus, but to become your own leader, become someone people want to talk about.

There's something about music, the giving, the attempting to be better every day. There are a lot of things that fall into that category, but music is just you and the instrument. It's not for everyone. But for the ones who really get that enjoyment, there's something magical that no one will ever be able to really put down in words.

I've kept learning all my life and it keeps paying off: dealing with people, communication, having your skills sharp, creativity that you learn at some point, patience, all those little things. Where are the diplomas? Time to hold out the hand. On January 23, 1990, at the Grand Avenue Bar in the Biltmore Hotel in downtown LA, Mayor Tom Bradley proclaimed "Buddy Collette Day" in Los Angeles. And more recently, Mayor Richard Riordan, on June 16, 1998, honored me as a "Los Angeles Living Cultural Treasure." Maybe these are kinds of diplomas. I didn't look for them, but I'll take them.

Music has also been important because it was one of the fields in which I saw black and whites work very closely together. And we helped to bring that about with the musicians' union amalgamation in Los Angles in 1953. We did it in music before it happened in a lot of other areas, and maybe music can now grow to another level. We seem to have hit a snag now and I think we need to go back to some of what we've learned in the past. The leaders, the bands, working together where there are blacks and whites in the band, and let people see that this can work. Today you've got a lot of kids thinking that it's okay to discriminate again, and I thought we were through with that.

In the early 1970s we tried, through the musicians' union, to deal with the racial division between Latinos and blacks that was becoming very serious and dangerous in the schools at places like Jefferson High School. Max Herman, who was President of Local 47 at that time, called in Eddie Cano, a fine pianist and arranger, Ruben Leon, a saxophonist and psychiatrist, and myself to talk about what could be done. We formed the Black–Brown Brotherhood Band and added Oscar Brashear, Britt Woodman, Poncho Sanchez, and David Trancosa. The point was to educate young people and to show performers from different cultures working together. It was a terrific band, and when we played in some very hot and difficult situations, racially, the music would cool everything down. When we left, the kids would be carrying our instruments and loving each other. It was a magical thing and Max knew what he was doing.

So by reaching back to some of these earlier experiences, we can move forward again. A lot of people are going to miss out unless they can change their feelings and take another look at it. All it means is just helping people and sharing. A great example of helping and sharing has been the Musicians Assistance Program at the union, started by Buddy Arnold to help musicians dealing with drug problems. Buddy had dealt with a serious problem himself, and because of that there was a lot of opposition. But we managed to get it going, and Buddy has done just a great job helping musicians with problems and providing guidance for young people.

A lot of people are realizing we need to be concerned, to work together, and many are doing it. A few years ago I worked a call for the ACLU at the Registry Hotel, about twelve hundred people. I had a seven- or eight-piece band with a singer. It's become that big and it's the place to be. Within a radius of ten feet in front of us there was Lloyd Bridges and his two sons, Beau and Jeff. Barbra Streisand, Jane Fonda, Cybil Shepherd were right there. John McTernan, the big lawyers, were there. I've seen it grow so big in about twenty years. So the fighting I've done has been mainly with the instrument. "Hey, go, gang. I can lend my name and I can bring a band for you or we can help you raise funds." I'm right with them. They said, "We don't do anything without you." And that's nice to know.

One night at the Registry Hotel, Cesar Chavez and Dolores Huerta were the speakers. Dolores spoke and talked about how they beat her, and the many struggles people have gone through. It was like, "Hey, this is the place to be," getting the real stories and asking, "Where are we as a people? Is it really getting better?" Not that we can solve everything, but, man, you sure have to be working together. It was beautiful to see people, who were willing to get up and talk, just lay it on the line without being afraid. During the late forties and the McCarthy period, you'd get up and say something like that, and some people would be hauling you away.

Unfortunately, many gains of the sixties and seventies didn't last. The music life has become a lot harder now. The eighties were not as good as the sixties or the seventies. There isn't as much work around the studios. Blacks aren't working there as they used to, and maybe won't again in TV and movies. I don't think the kind of pressure that we exerted in 1965, 1974, 1975, will ever be as effective again. A lot changed during the Reagan administration in the eighties. Attitudes changed. It's like we're going back, even though we have gone forward in some ways.

These concerns are a growing thing with me, and it's bigger than me being just a great player and then not knowing what's happening with people. Do we have a future here with the unions? Do we have a future in life? At a certain point we have to ask ourselves the question: "Did we really do what we could in the best way?" Hopefully, I'll always be able to answer, "I think so" or, "I understood what was needed, other than just making the kind of money I wanted." When my book comes out, it won't be talking about how much music I know. What it will say is that I've lived it. And when you've lived something, it shows in your movements.

Discography

In 1985 Coen Hofmann published *Man of Many Parts: A Discography of Buddy Collette* (Amsterdam: MICROGRAPHY). That volume thoroughly covered Buddy's recording history in almost one hundred pages, and consequently will not be duplicated here. The following represents Buddy's work since that time on CD. Selections from previously issued work that have been made available in that format are also included, though for reasons of space this is a partial listing. Buddy's numerous appearances as a sideman, now offered on CD, include sessions with Hamiet Bluiett, Miles Davis, Dizzy Gillespie, Benny Goodman, Quincy Jones, Barney Kessel, Lyle "Spud" Murphy, Zoot Sims, Jimmy Smith, Stanley Turrentine, and Gerald Wilson.

An asterisk after the title * indicates original compositions by Buddy Collette.

I. LEADER

1. Buddy Collette Quartet in *Central Avenue Sounds; Jazz in Los Angeles (1921–1956)*. Rhino R2 75872, 1999.
   Originally recorded in Los Angeles, 1948.
   Collette (as), Jimmie O'Brien (p), Harper Crosby (b), Chuck Thompson (d)

   It's April*
   Collette*

2. Buddy Collette. *Man of Many Parts*. Contemporary OJCCD-239–2 (C-3522), 1992.
   Originally recorded in Los Angeles, February 13, 24, April 17, 1956.

Gerald Wilson (tp), David Wells (btp, tb), Collette (as, ts, cl, fl), William Green (as), Jewell Grant (bs), Ernie Freeman (p), Red Callender (b), Max Albright (d); Gerald Wiggins (p), Gene Wright (b), Bill Richmond (d); Barney Kessel (g), Ernie Freeman (p), Joe Comfort (b), Larry Bunker (d).

> Cycle*
> Makin' Whoopee
> Ruby
> St. Andrew's Place Blues*
> Cheryl Ann*
> Sunset Drive*
> Jazz City Blues*
> Slappy's Tune*
> Frenesi
> Santa Monica*
> Jungle Pipe*
> Zan*

3. The Buddy Collette-Chico Hamilton Sextet. *Tanganyika*. VSOP #20 CD, 1993.
   Originally recorded in Hollywood, October 11, 1956.
   John Anderson (tp), Collette (reeds), Gerald Wiggins (p), Jim Hall (g), Curtis Counce (b), Hamilton (d)

> Green Dream*
> It's You*
> A Walk on the Veldt*
> How Long Has This Been Going On?
> The Blindfold Test
> Jungle Pogo Stick*
> Tanganyika*
> Wagnervous
> And So Is Love
> Coming Back For More

4. *Nice Day with Buddy Collette*. Contemporary OJCCD-747–2 (C-3531), 1992.
   Originally recorded in Los Angeles, November 6, 29, 1956, February 18, 1957.

Collette (as, ts, cl, fl), Don Friedman (p), Dick Shreve (p), Calvin Jackson (p), John Goodman (b), Leroy Vinnegar (b), Bill Dolney (d), Shelly Manne (d)

A Nice Day*
There Will Never Be Another You
Minor Deviation
Over The Rainbow
Change It*
Moten Swing
I'll Remember April
Blues For Howard*
Fall Winds*
Buddy Boo*

5. Buddy Collette Quartet and Quintet. *Tasty Dish*. Fresh Sound FSR-CD 213, 1996.
   Originally recorded in Los Angeles, November 19, 1956, May 14, 15, 1957.
   Collette (as, ts, cl, fl), Dick Shreve (p), John Goodman (b), Bill Dolney (d); Gerald Wiggins (p), Howard Roberts (g), Eugene Wright (b), Bill Richmond (d); Shreve (p), Wright (b), Richmond (d)

Makin' Whoopee
Fall Wind*
I'll Remember April
Tasty Dish*
I Still Love You*
Mrs. Potts
You Better Go Now
Orlando Blues*
Soft Touch*
Old School
Debbie

6. The Buddy Collette Quintet. *Buddy's Best*. Ace Records CDBOP 020, 1996.
   Originally recorded in Los Angeles, 1957.

Gerald Wilson (tp), Collette (as, ts, cl, fl), Al Viola (g), Wilfred Middlebrook (b), Earl Palmer (d)

Soft Touch*
Walkin' Willie*
Changes*
My Funny Valentine
The Cute Monster*
Orlando Blues*
Blue Sands*
It's You*

7. Herbie Mann & Buddy Collette. *Flute Fraternity*. VSOP #38 CD, 1997.
Originally recorded in Hollywood, July 1957.
Herbie Mann (fl, afl, cl, ts), Collette (af, afl, cl, as, ts), Jimmy Rowles (p), Buddy Clark (b), Mel Lewis (d)

Herbie's Buddy
Perdido
Baubles, Bangles and Beads
Give a Little Whistle
Here's Pete
Theme from "Theme From"
Nancy with the Laughing Face
Morning After

8. Buddy Collette. *Jazz Loves Paris*. Specialty OJCCD-1764–2 (SP-5002), 1991.
Originally recorded in Hollywood, January 24, 1958.
Frank Rosolino (tb), Collette (as, ts, cl, fl), Red Callender (tuba), Howard Roberts (g), Red Mitchell (b), Bill Richmond (d), Bill Douglass (d)

I Love Paris
Pigalle
La Vie En Rose
Darling, Je Vous Aime Beaucoup
Mam'selle
C'est Si Bon
Domino

Song From "Moulin Rouge" (Where Is Your Heart)
The Last Time I Saw Paris
Under Paris Skies
Darling, Je Vous Aime Beaucoup (Take 1 – Alt.)
Mam'selle (Take 2 – Alt.)
The Last Time I Saw Paris (Take 3 – Alt.)
La Vie En Rose (Take 1 – Alt.)

9. *The Buddy Collette Quintet with Guest Vocalist Irene Kral.* Studio West #104CD, 1990.
Originally recorded in Hollywood, 1962.
Collette (as, ts, cl, fl), Jack Wilson (p), Al Viola (g), Jimmy Bond (b), Bill Goodwin (d), Kral (voc)

A Taste Of Fresh Air*
Hunt And Peck*
Emaline's Theme*
The Meaning Of The Blues
Laura
Just Friends
There Will Never Be Another You
Spring Can Really Hang You Up The Most
Tenderly
Nobody Else But Me
Road Trip*
Detour Ahead
Soft Touch*
It's A Wonderful World

10. Buddy Collette Quintet feat. James Newton. *Flute Talk.* Soul Note 121 165–2, 1989.
Recorded July 4, 5, 1988.
Collette (as, cl, fl), Newton (fl), Geri Allen (p), Jaribu Shahid (b), Gianpiero Prina (d)

Magali*
Blues In Torrance*
Richmond in Acropolis
It's You*
Crystal*

Andre*
Flute Talk*
Roshanda*

11. Buddy Collette. *Jazz for Thousand Oaks*. UFO-BASS #002, 1996.
Recorded June 2, 1996.
Al Aarons (tp, flghn), George Bohanon (tb), Collette (as, ts, cl, fl), Sam Most (as, ts, afl), Ronnell Bright (p, voc), Al Viola (g), Richard Simon (b), Ndugu Chancler (d)

Villes Ville Is The Place, Man
Veda*
Sea Mist
Jazz For Thousand Oaks*
Talk About Loving You
Andre*
Hunt And Peck*

12. *Buddy Collette Big Band in Concert*. BRIDGE 9096, 2000.
Recorded in Washington, D.C., June 6, 1996.
Collette (dir.), trumpets: Al Aarons, Ronald Barrows, Anne King, Nolan Shaheed; trombones: Les Benedict, George Bohanon, Garnett Brown, Jr., Maurice Spears, Britt Woodman; woodwinds: Steven Carr, Jackie Kelson, Ann Patterson, John Stephens, Louis Taylor, Jr., Ernie Fields, Jr. (on "Buddy Boo"); Fred Katz (cello), Al Viola (g), Richard Simon (b), Ndugu Chancler (d), Chico Hamilton (d on "Buddy Boo").

Magali*
Andre*
Mr. and Mrs. Goodbye*
Blues Number Four*
Jazz by the Bay*
Blues in Torrance*
Point Fermin from "Friendships Suite"*
Buddy Boo*

II. SIDEMAN

1. Benny Carter, Wilbert Baranco, Gerald Wilson, Jimmy Mundy and Their Orchestras.
   Groovin' High in L.A. (1946). HEP CD 15, 1992.
   Originally recorded in January 1946.
   Wilbert Baranco Orchestra: Hobart Dotson (tp), Karl George (tp), Snooky Young (tp), Howard McGhee (tp – possibly), Ralph Bledsoe or Henry Coker (tb), Melba Liston (tb), George Washington (tb), Britt Woodman (tb), Buddy Collette (as), Jack Kelson (as), Maurice Simon (ts), Lucky Thompson (ts), Eugene Porter (bs), Baranco (p), Buddy Harper (g), Charles Mingus (b), Earl Watkins (d)

   > Bugle Call Rag
   > Night And Day
   > Everytime I Think Of You
   > Baranco Boogie

2. Baron Mingus and His Octet in *Central Avenue Sounds; Jazz in Los Angeles (1921–1956)*. Rhino R2 75872, 1999.
   Originally recorded in Los Angeles, 1946.
   Karl George (tp), John Anderson (tp), Britt Woodman (tb), Collette (cl, as), William Woodman, Jr. (ts), Lady Will Carr (p), Mingus (b), Eugene Porter (b), Oscar Bradley (d)

   > Bedspread*
   > Pipe Dream

3. Charles Mingus in *Central Avenue Sounds; Jazz in Los Angeles (1921–1956)*. Rhino R2 75872, 1999.
   Originally recorded in Los Angeles, 1949.
   Collette (cl, as), unknown (p), Mingus (b), unknown (d)

   > Mingus Fingers
   > These Foolish Things

4. Joe Swanson Orchestra feat. Wardell Gray in *Central Avenue Sounds; Jazz in Los Angeles (1921–1956)*. Rhino R2 75872, 1999.
   Originally recorded in Los Angeles, 1952.

John Anderson (tp), Jimmy Cheatham (tb), John "Streamline" Ewing (tb), Buddy Collette (as, fl), Swanson (ts), Gray (ts), Jewell Grant (bs), Gerald Wiggins (p), Irving Ashby (g), David Bryant (b), Bill Douglass (d)

East Of The Sun
Thrust

5. *The Complete Pacific Jazz Recordings of the Chico Hamilton Quintet.* Mosaic MD6–175, 1997.
Originally recorded in Los Angeles and Long Beach, August 4, 23, November 11, 1955, January 4, February 10, 13, 1956, January 9, 12, 1959
Collette (as, ts, cl, fl), Fred Katz (cello), Jim Hall (g), Carson Smith (b), Chico Hamilton (d). Add Paul Horn (as, cl, fl) to '59 sessions.

A Nice Day*
My Funny Valentine
Blue Sands*
The Sage
The Morning After
I Want To Be Happy
Spectacular
Free Form
Walking Carson Blues
Buddy Boo*
Gone With The Wind
Topsy
Undecided
My Old Flame
The Saint
It Don't Mean A Thing
Stella By Starlight
Caravan
Tea For Two
Fast Flute*
Change It*
Cute Little Deal
A Mood

This Is Your Day*
I'll Keep Loving You
Crazy Rhythm
Jonalah
Chrissie
The Wind
Gone Lover (When Your Lover Has Gone)
The Ghost*
Sleepy Slept Here*
Taking A Chance On Love
The Squimp
Topsy
Sleep
Medley: Take The A Train/Perdido
Everything But You
I'm Just A Lucky So And So
Azure
I'm Beginning To See The Light
In A Mellotone
Just A-Sittin' And A-Rockin'
In A Sentimental Mood
Day Dream
It Don't Mean A Thing

6. Charles Mingus. *The Complete Town Hall Concert*. Blue Note
   CDP 7243, 1994.
   Originally recorded in New York, October 12, 1962.
   Snooky Young (tp), Ernie Royal (tp), Richard Williams (tp),
   Clark Terry (tp), Eddie Armour (tp), Lonnie Hillyer (tp), Rolf
   Ericson (tp), Quentin Jackson (tb), Britt Woodman (tb), Jimmy
   Cleveland (tb), Willie Dennis (tb), Eddie Bert (tb), Paul Faulise
   (tb), Eric Dolphy (as), Charles McPherson (as), Charlie Mariano
   (as), Collette (as), Romeo Penque (ob), Zoot Sims (ts), George
   Berg (ts), Jerome Richardson (bs), Pepper Adams (bs), Danny
   Bank (cbcl), Jaki Byard (p), Toshiko Akiyoshi (p), Les Spann
   (g), Milt Hinton (b), Mingus (b), Dannie Richmond (d), Warren
   Smith (vb, perc), Grady Tate (perc)

   Freedom (Parts 1 and 2)

Osmotin'
Epitaph (Part 1)
Peggy's Blue Skylight
Epitaph (Part 2)
My Search
Portrait
Duke's Choice
Please Don't Come Back From The Moon
In A Mellotone
Epitaph (Part 1 alt.)

7. The Original Chico Hamilton Quintet. *Reunion*. Soul Note 121191-2, 1991.
   Recorded in Milan, Italy, June 28, 29, 1989.
   Collette (as, cl, fl), Fred Katz (cello), Jim Hall (g), Carson Smith (b), Chico Hamilton (d, voc)
   I Want to Be Happy
   Delightful, Charming and Cool
   Brushing with B* (with Chico Hamilton)
   Ain't Nobody Calling Me
   Magali*
   Shirley
   Conversation* (with Chico Hamilton)
   These Are the Dues
   Dreams of Youth
   Five Friends* (with the rest of the quintet)
   Reunion*

8. Joe Rosenberg's Affinity. *A Tribute to Eric Dolphy with Buddy Collette*. Music & Arts CD-939, 1996.
   Recorded in Berkeley, CA, March 24, 25, 1995.
   Collette (as, fl), Joe Rosenberg (ss), Rob Sudduth (ts), Michael Silverman (b), Bobby Lurie (d)

   Bee Vamp
   Booker's Waltz
   Ode To Charlie Parker
   Fire Waltz
   Mendacity
   So Long Eric

9. Richard Simon. *Covering the Basses*. UFO-BASS #003, 1997. Recorded in Hollywood, CA, October 29–30, November 7, 1997. Collette (as, ts, fl), Gil Bernal (ts), Art Hillery (p, org), Al Viola (g), Simon (b), Johnny Kirkwood (d)

> Melatonin
> Theme From "Poultry-geist"
> Ray's Idea
> Unit Seven
> What's New
> For Carl
> Detour Ahead
> In A Hurry
> Tricrotism
> Blues For Stephanie
> The Backbone
> Goodbye Porkpie Hat

III. SPOKEN WORD

1. *Buddy Collette – A Jazz Audio Biography*. Issues ISS CD 005, 1994.

Index

Index

207

Index

Index

Index

213

Index

214